MATTHEW: SAGE THEOLOGIAN

D1513860

They shall name him Emmanuel,
which means, 'God is with us'…

And remember, I am with you always,
to the end of the age.
Mt 1:23; 28:30

Wilfrid J. Harrington, O.P.

Matthew: Sage Theologian
The Jesus of Matthew

the columba press

First published, 1998, by
che columba press
55A Spruce Avenue, Stillorgan Industrial Park,
Blackrock, Co Dublin

Cover by Bill Bolger
Origination by The Columba Press
Printed in Ireland by Colour Books Ltd, Dublin

ISBN 1 85607 245 2

Contents

Introduction

The Synoptic Gospels are notably similar. All the more, then, their obvious distinctive differences underline the individuality of the three evangelists. Already, in this trio, we have proof of the exuberant pluralism of New Testament theology and, more specifically, of its christology. Mark, Luke, Matthew are Christians all of them. They do not speak with one 'official' voice. They witness, powerfully, to the wondrous richness of Jesus Christ. I have, already, sketched the Jesus-perception of Mark and Luke.[1] Now it is the turn of Matthew.

Matthew's portrait of Jesus is coloured by two factors. He is a committed Jewish-Christian, wholly convinced that Jesus is the Messiah of Jewish hope and expectation. As member of a predominantly Jewish-Christian community, he is grieved by the antagonism of contemporary official Judaism. And, his Jesus, while prophet and healer, is more firmly in the line of the sages of Israel. He is, preeminently, Teacher.

These are emphases. All New Testament writers are committed disciples of the one Jesus Christ. The variety is heartening. It is a variety that needs to be stressed in our day. There are, of course, basic principles. But the New Testament shows that 'in my Father's house there are many dwelling places' (Jn 14:2). Variety is the spice of life. Pluralism should be a marked feature of authentic Christianity. It is, unquestionably, a feature of New Testament Christianity.

CHAPTER 1

Matthew

*Every scribe who has been trained for the kingdom of heaven is like the
master of a household who brings out of his treasure what is new and
what is old* (Mt 13:52)

In the decade AD 80-90 a Jewish Christian theologian – we name
him 'Matthew' – made a synthesis of Mark and 'Q' (a collection of
Jesus' sayings). He had, besides, access to other material (conven-
tionally designated 'M'). His community, likely based at Antioch in
Syria, was in a crisis situation. It had been a wholly Jewish community, tolerated by Judaism. But now, after the destruction of
Jerusalem in 70 AD, and the reorganisation of a shattered Judaism,
it had broken with official Judaism. As a Jewish Christian, writing
out of and for a Jewish Christian community, Matthew, like all
Jews, had to face up to a radical challenge to Jewish identity. There
were stark questions: Where is Israel now? Who is heir to the biblical promises? We will, through the book, concentrate on his
answer. First, however, we note that the broad Jewish response
took two main shapes: apocalyptic and early rabbinic Judaism (or
formative Judaism).

APOCALYPTIC

It is generally assumed that apocalyptic springs from the experience of alienation, or arises in times of crisis – it may be perceived
crisis. An apocalyptic group sets up its own symbolic universe or
world-view: a system of thought within which it can live its life.
Usually it does so in protest against the dominant society with
which it is in conflict. The group has a painful experience of alienation, which may be due to a quarrel with the power-group within
its own society. This would fit the situation of Matthew's community.
A Jewish-Christian group, they were alienated from their ethnic
brothers and sisters. They were involved in a 'civil war' – which

goes far to explain the sad virulence of Matthew 23. The tragedy is that here, as with depressing regularity throughout 'Christian' history, Jesus has been dragged into Christian squabbles.

Two major Jewish apocalypses responded to the 70 AD crisis: 4 Ezra and 2 Baruch – both roughly from about the same time as Matthew. Both must acknowledge Roman victory. Their verdict: it is ephemeral. God has the last word. His Messiah will shortly emerge to reverse the present tragic state of Zion.

Formative Judaism

The apocalyptic view was bolstered by another response. Vindication was certain, but it had to be prepared for. It might be hastened by faithful observance of the Law: revelation of God's will. This is the contribution of another movement after 70 AD which was formative of subsequent Judaism. The three pillars of Israel had been Torah, Temple, Land. Now land and temple were gone; Torah alone remained. The Pharisees had been stalwart champions of Torah; now they came into their own. In their view, loyal, total, observance of Torah was the way of hope, was the only and adequate answer to the crisis. Only by way of meticulous observance of the Law could God's promises to his people be fulfilled. When the way had been prepared, God's Anointed One would appear to restore the fortunes of Zion.

> Matthew shared the apocalyptic hope of 4 Ezra and 2 Baruch. But Matthew identified the Messiah as Jesus of Nazareth and took Jesus' interpretation of the Law as the proper guide to behaviour in the present. Matthew shared the practical agenda of formative Judaism on many points. But he rejected the Pharisees' traditions and interpretations in favour of the teachings of Jesus. Thus Matthews's Gospel emerges as a Jewish Christian response to the events of 70 AD.[2]

MATTHEW

The Jewish Christian, Matthew, wrote a Christian gospel. For him, as for Paul, the hope of Israel was in Jesus Christ. His post-70 AD situation was not that of Paul. The Apostle was wholly convinced that Israel had not been, because it never could be, set aside (see Rom 9-11). Matthew, immersed in the conflict situation after 70 AD, was not so sanguine. For him, official Judaism was the enemy. In his day, the powerful priesthood had been obliterated. Pharisees were his target, his *bête noire*. His polemical stance is understandable in the context of his situation. Taken out of context, it has proved disastrous. His chapter 23, above all, has led to a practically universal Christian characterisation of Pharisees as 'hypocrites' – grossly unfair. And that seeming self-curse, 'His blood be on us and on our children', (27:25) has occasioned brutal persecution of Jews throughout Christian history. There has been a sad failing in perception. In Matthew's situation ethnic Jews, Christian and non-Christian were in conflict. There was no love lost. But this is not anti-Semitism.

Matthew does not hide his bias. He does *not* like the Pharisees. One feels that what more seriously disturbed him was discernment of 'pharisees' within his own community. It is, in some way, ironical that this traditionally solidly ecclesiastical gospel is, really, subversive of 'ecclesiasticism'. I have often thought that a high-point of ecclesiastical 'hard-neck' is the proclamation of Mt 23:1-10 at Sunday Mass – without embarrassment or apology! When one really looks at this passage, and contrasts the practice of the Christian church over the centuries, one must feel some dismay.

THE GOSPEL

The Sources

The great majority of New Testament scholars work with the Two-Source Theory: Mark is our earliest gospel; Matthew and Luke have used Mark and another hypothetical text known as Q (from the German *Quelle*, 'source'). The theory accounts, very reasonably, for the large amount of gospel material shared by Matthew and Luke. As well, each evangelist has material proper to himself: for instance, the Infancy Narratives (Mt 1-2; Lk 1-2). The source Q, a Greek document, was, almost wholly, a collection of sayings and parables. The outline of it is found, most persuasively, in Luke. It is strongly sapiential in tone and carries a notable eschatological emphasis. By his inclusion of Q material, Matthew gave a firm emphasis to Jesus as a teacher. Of course, the hypothetical Q document is not extant. This has not hindered some from presenting assured reconstructions. Nor, indeed, from going on to describe the Q community, with a confident sketch of its theology. The existence of a Q document is the hypothesis that best explains the remarkable non-Marcan connections between Matthew and Luke. But that shadowy Q should be left in its decent anonymity.

The Structure

Over a teaching and research career of more than forty years, I have become increasingly sceptical of scholarly plans of biblical writings which purport to have discerned the literary map of a biblical author and provide the key that unlocks his purpose. Ironically, one finds that a convincingly attractive scheme is, very soon, blown apart by the next contender. Of course, some incontestable features will emerge. One cannot ignore that the five great discourses are distinctive of Matthew. One wonders if we should push far beyond that fact. In any case, I am content to work with a broad plan that does not appear to do violence to the gospel. I might even claim that it is, in the main, the route followed by most commentators.

The centre of the gospel – the public ministry – is built up of five major sections, each with a pattern of narrative plus discourse (chapters 2-25). To this, the Infancy Narrative is prologue or introduction, the Passion Narrative conclusion or climax.

Introduction: Infancy Narrative 1-2
I. Proclamation of the Kingdom 3-7
    Preliminary Manifestation 3-4
    Sermon on the Mount 5-7

II. Mission in Galilee 8-10
    Healings 8-9
    Mission Sermon 10

III. The Hidden Kingdom 11-13
    Opposition and Division 11-12
    Sermon in Parables 13

IV. The Kingdom Develops 14-18
    Formation of Disciples 14-17
    Sermon on the Church 18

V. Towards the Passion 19-23
  Mounting Opposition 19-23
  Judgment Sermon 24-25

Climax: Passion Death, Resurrection 26-28

However one seeks to structure it, this gospel is, before anything else, a proclamation of Jesus of Nazareth, *risen* Lord, present and active in the Christian community. Matthew acknowledged Jesus as Prophet and Healer. What, in our respect, marks him off from the other synoptists is his emphasis on Jesus as Teacher or Sage. It is a matter of emphasis. But, because the purpose of this book is to portray Jesus from Matthew's perspective, focus will be on the discourses – the sermons. Beforehand, one offers a sketch of Matthew's theology.

THEOLOGY

Kingdom of Heaven

Hope for the coming of God's kingdom was current in Matthew's day. It was firmly present in apocalyptic (e.g. Daniel, 4 Ezra, 2 Baruch) and in the Qumran community. The hope was that God's rule would become so manifest that all creation would acknowledge God as sole and supreme Lord. It is summed up in the Lord's Prayer: 'Your kingdom come. Your will be done on earth as it is in heaven' (Mt 6:10). Matthew's customary expression, 'kingdom of heaven' is a feature of his Jewishness: 'heaven' is a reverential avoidance of a too frequent use of 'God'. What is more distinctive of Matthew's treatment of the kingdom is the decisive role of Jesus. For him, Jesus is the one who ushered in the Rule of God. It is already present in his ministry. His followers will help to make it a reality by hearkening to his word.

Christology

To speak of Matthew's 'christology' is to refer to the entire portrayal of Jesus conveyed by this narrative. A gospel's 'christology' is the summation of the meaning it assigns to the life, ministry, destiny, and person of Jesus. Unlike systematic theology where a particular 'christology' is developed in an orderly and logical fashion, the narrative theology of a gospel creates a christology by means of the distinctive features of its portrayal of Jesus. As such, virtually every aspect of the gospel relates to its christology.[3]

One endorses this statement, wholeheartedly. In a book subtitled 'The Jesus of Matthew' it is obvious that christology must be a major concern. Here it will suffice to indicate some of Matthew's contributions. Like Luke, his infancy narrative (indeed, beforehand, his genealogy) declares at the outset who, in his estimation, this Jesus is. He is 'son of David and son of Abraham', wholly of his people. His name Yeshua ('God saves') proclaimed his mission: 'he will save his people from their sins' (1:21). His status is nutshelled in the prophetic name Emmanuel – 'God with us' (see 28:20).

A feature of Matthew's gospel is his use of Old Testament fulfilment quotations ('All this took place to fulfil what the Lord had spoken through the prophets…'). He had recognised the applicability of particular Old Testament texts to particular incidents in Jesus' career. In word and deed, Jesus fulfilled the Scriptures (see 1:23; 2:15, 18, 23; 4:15-16; 8:17; 12:18-21; 13:35; 21:5; 26:56; 27:9-10). This places Jesus in an unassailable position as a radical interpreter of Scripture (5:17-48).

Matthew uses the standard christological titles: Son of David, Messiah, Son of Man, Son of God, Lord. He attaches to these titles his distinctive cachet. His Son of David (1:1) is the one who went out of his way to help the no-accounts (20:29-34). As the Servant (see Is 53:4) he took upon himself our infirmities and diseases (Mt 8:17). The Messiah of Matthew is healer indeed. He is, more obviously, teacher. As wisdom teacher he is, ultimately, personified Wisdom (11:28-30; see Sirach 5:23-30). As Son of Man he stands (rather, sits!) as definitive Judge (Mt 25).

Ethics

To qualify for membership in the Kingdom one must do the will of the Father (7:21). The basis of Jewish morality was the 'ten words' (Ex 20:1-21; Deut 5:6-21). For Christians it is no longer the norm. Now the yardstick is: 'these words of mine' (Mt 7:24, 26). Matthew's Jewish Christians must make their choice: will they live by Torah or by the word of the risen Lord? Looking back over Christian history one must acknowledge that the emphasis has been on the *thou shalt not* of the commandments. Jesus' clarion call to radical freedom had been stifled by ecclesiastical 'prudence' almost from the start (see the Pastorals). At first sight, Matthew might seem to bolster that 'respectable' approach. Read more perceptively, this gospel will emerge as revolutionary. The structure may be sedate. The message is challenging. 'Be perfect as your heavenly Father is perfect' (Mt 5:48). It is the obligation of every Christian.

CHURCH

The narrative section Mt 11-12 opens with a question of the Baptist: 'Are you the one who is to come, or are we to wait for another?' The evangelist manifestly expects his readers to ask themselves the same question. But Matthew believed that a decision regarding Jesus necessarily involved a decision concerning his church. An authentic commitment to Jesus was possible only within the context of membership in his community.

In this gospel it becomes quite difficult to distinguish between the disciples and the community (or church) because in Matthew's eyes they blend into one. This is evident in the instruction given to the disciples in chapter 18. It is here that Matthew brings together his significant ideas on the church: true greatness (vv 1-4), scandal (5-10), concern for the vulnerable (12-14), brotherly correction and authentic authority (15-18), fellowship in prayer (19-20), gracious forgiveness (21-35).

The church is a family of children of the Father. Jesus is dynamically present in his church. He is with his followers, present in his missionaries (10:40), in all in need (25:35-45), in all received in his name (18:5). But Matthew, too, sees the community as a ship beaten by the waves, as he shows in his story of the stilling of the storm (8:23-27). In his gospel this episode becomes a paradigm of discipleship for, even more than in Mark, his boat becomes a 'ship of the Church', and the cry 'Save, Lord' is at once a prayer and a confession of discipleship.

CONCLUSION

It is arguable that the earliest Matthean community viewed itself as a sectarian group of the perfect – a reformed covenant group which cast Jesus as a reforming prophet. Hence his demand: 'Unless your righteousness exceeds that of the scribes and Pharisees, you will never enter the kingdom of heaven' (5:20). Later, influenced by the fall of Jerusalem and by a firm opening to the Gentiles, there was a radical reappraisal. Whereas for the early community Jesus was perceived as a prophetic figure stressing perfection and separation from evil, for the later community he had become covenant leader of the new covenant people of Jew and Gentile, urging toleration, forgiveness and mercy. This is the Matthean Jesus of our concern. Matthew's portrait will stand out more sharply against the broader gospel picture. The following chapter sketches that background.

CHAPTER 2

Jesus

For we do not have a high priest who is unable to sympathise with our weaknesses, but we have one who in every respect has been tested as we are, yet without sin… Therefore he had to become like his brothers and sisters in every respect. (Heb 4:15; 1:17)

Our immediate concern is the Jesus of Matthew – I have earlier looked at the Jesus of Mark and of Luke.[4] But, *Jesus* is one. This chapter might be a salutary reminder as it sketches, in broad strokes, a gospel portrait of Jesus. The New Testament makes clear that, following on initial varied perceptions of him, Christian faith came to focus on the *risen* Jesus and on his vital presence among them as Spirit. This risen Lord and Jesus of Nazareth are one and the same. I, deliberately, concentrate on the one 'like his brothers and sisters in every respect' (Heb 2:17).

'God was in Christ, reconciling the world to himself' (2 Cor 5:19). This is, arguably, the very best christological statement, and it weds christology with soteriology. Where Jesus is, there is God; and God is there for us. But Jesus of Nazareth is the thoroughly human person who was 'born of woman' (Gal 4:4), who lived in our world, who died, horribly, on a cross. We meet God in Jesus. The author of Hebrews has told us in no uncertain terms: 'Long ago God spoke to our ancestors in many and various ways by the prophets.' This is revelation of God indeed, but fragmentary, and mediated through his servants. 'In these past days he has spoken to us by a Son… he is the reflection of God's glory and the exact imprint of God's very being' (Heb 1:1-3).

If Jesus bears the stamp of God's very being, he does so as a human person, like us in all things. Jesus tells us what God is like. Jesus is

God's summons to us, God's challenge to us. We can say, truly, that God is love; but we have no idea what God's love is in itself. In Jesus we see God's love in action. We learn that God is a God who is with us in our suffering and in our death. We are sure of it because of the suffering and death of Jesus.

In Jesus, God has shown himself in human form: 'he is the image of the invisible God' (Col 1:15). In practice, we have slipped quickly past this human aspect. We have turned, instead, to a 'divine icon' comfortably free of any trait of the critical prophet. We have consigned Jesus to his heavenly home. Jesus of Nazareth is a very uncomfortable person to have around, a constant challenge. We look to this Jesus.

JESUS OF NAZARETH

The object of Christian faith is the person of Jesus Christ who once lived, briefly, in the first century AD and now lives on in the Father's presence. The subject matter of the gospels is this Jesus Christ. The gospels, at once historical and theological, proclaim Jesus of Nazareth as the Christ, the definitive revelation of God. The proclaimed Jesus is a construct of Christian theological and spiritual imagination aimed at eliciting a faith response. The proclamation embraces strictly historical elements (e.g. Jesus' death on the cross) and theological interpretation in terms of biblical categories (e.g. ascent to God's right hand).

The real or actual Jesus is the glorified Saviour alive in our midst. He will always be shrouded in mystery. The total reality of any person is unknowable to human discernment – how much more the reality of the Risen One. The gospels present us with 'the earthly Jesus.' The historical Jesus is not the real Jesus, but only a fragmentary hypothetical reconstruction of him by modern means of research. But this reconstruction is of immense importance – particularly in our day. Jesus is an appealing and a challenging figure.

The historical Jesus is not coextensive with the Jesus of the gospel narratives. There is much in the gospel narratives that is not historical. The gospel picture is 'accurate' not in the sense that it is exact in detail but that it is truth-bearing. It is the acceptance of it by the

early believing community that guarantees the substantial truth of
the gospel account. The gospel Jesus is more than the historical
Jesus: the gospel presents not only history but the transhistorical,
not only fact but theological interpretation. On the other hand, the
ecclesiastical proclamation of the Jesus-image is often less than, is
unfaithful to, the historical Jesus in which the image is rooted. This
is a further reason for investigation of and discernment of the historical Jesus. We must not shrink from facing up to the 'dangerous
memory'.

THE HISTORICAL JESUS

Jesus of Nazareth was a first-century AD Jew who began, lived and
ended his short life in Palestine, a minor province of the Roman
Empire. Our information about him, by historical standards, is
meagre. Apart from two brief statements, by the Jewish historian
Flavius Josephus and the Roman historian Tacitus respectively, our
sources for knowledge of the historical Jesus are the canonical
gospels alone.

Around 7-4 BC, that is, toward the close of the reign of Herod the
Great, a Jewish boy, to be named Jesus (Yeshua), was born, either in
Bethlehem of Judaea or Nazareth of Galilee. His mother was named
Mary (Miryam), his putative father Joseph (Yosef). He grew up in
Nazareth and was known as 'the Nazarene'. His native language
was Aramaic; he would have had a practical command of Greek. It
is highly likely that he was literate; as a boy he would have been
taught in the village synagogue. Like Joseph, Jesus was a *tektón* –
most probably a carpenter. In a small village Joseph's would have
been the only carpenter shop; the family would have had a frugally
comfortable life-style. Jesus lived and worked in the quiet obscurity
of that Galilean village until, in his early thirties, there came a radical change.

Disciple of the Baptist

The starting-point for any account of the ministry of Jesus of
Nazareth is his encounter with John the Baptist: the call which Jesus
heard when he was baptised by John and to which he responded.
By submitting to baptism Jesus became, in effect, a disciple of the

Baptist. Here the evidence is compelling; unexpectedly, perhaps, the evidence of the Fourth Gospel.

The baptism of Jesus by John is certainly historical – note the embarrassment of Mt 3:13-15. We look to the implication of it. In the first place, it indicated a fundamental change in Jesus' life: he became a disciple of the Baptist. He had come to know the eschatological message of John and showed, by his adherence, his basic acceptance of it. He submitted to John's baptism as a seal on his decision to change his manner of life. Hitherto, he had been a village carpenter; henceforth he would be proclaimer of the word. He would preach *metanoia*, a radical change of heart, in a wholehearted striving to renew Israel. The baptism launched him on a road that would eventually lead to the cross – though, surely, this prospect did not then appear on his horizon.

Decision

Jesus, baptised by John, began his ministry as disciple of the Baptist. He went on to launch his own distinctive mission. This was a major decision which involved other decisions. He was thoroughly convinced of his calling. He had, however, to work out for himself how his mission would be carried through; he had to learn how, perfectly, to represent his Abba. To make the Abba known: that was his role. The temptation stories, placed, dramatically, by Matthew and Luke before the opening of his mission, incorporate decisions he was to arrive at throughout his ministry.

The letter to the Hebrews tells us that Jesus was 'one who in every respect has been tested as we are, yet without sin' (4:15). How are we to understand that 'without sin'? Is it *non posse peccare*? or *posse non peccare*? That is: incapable of sin? or able not to sin? In the past, the preference was for the former: Jesus was wholly incapable of sin. But that makes testing or temptation pointless. The author of Hebrews is quite sure that the testing was very real. Paul has the same view. This is brought out, splendidly, by C.H. Dodd in his comment on Rom 6:9-10 – 'death no longer has dominion over him (Christ); the death he died, he died to sin once for all.'

The sense of these words must be understood from other passages in which Paul speaks of the life and death of Jesus in relation to the condition of the world. Mankind was bound in the servitude of Sin, established in the 'flesh.' Thus the natural, flesh-and-blood life of man was the territory, so to speak, of Sin, and all dwellers on that territory Sin claimed as his own. Christ, by his incarnation, became a denizen of 'the flesh.' Sin put in its claim. In other words, Jesus was tempted to sin, as we are all tempted, in such forms as sin might take for one in his situation. But instead of yielding, and acknowledging Sin's dominion, as we all do, he rendered a perfect obedience to God... 'and became obedient to the point of death' (Phil 2:8). Jesus, in plain terms, died rather than sin; and so his death instead of being a sign of the victory of Sin over man's true nature, was a sign of the complete rout of Sin in a decisive engagement.[5]

Luke and Matthew also believe that Jesus was really tested – that he had to make moral decisions: otherwise their temptation story is meaningless. In each of his three ripostes to 'the devil' Jesus cited texts from Deuteronomy, and these texts are the key to the meaning of each scene.

1. 'One does not live by bread alone' (Deut 8:3). Jesus had been challenged to provide food miraculously for himself, to use his authority as Son apart from the Father's design.

2. 'Do not put the Lord your God to the test' (6:16). Again, Jesus was challenged to use his power on his own behalf, this time to dazzle his contemporaries and conform to their image of a heaven-sent messiah.

3. 'Worship the Lord your God and serve only him' (6:13). Jesus was challenged to be wholly autonomous; to do things entirely his way. His firm decision was that if he is to have *exousia*, authority, he will have it from the Father alone. He will learn that his exercise of authority will ever be *diakonia*, service.

The temptations of Jesus are the ongoing temptations of Christians: to seek one's glory, even in religious matters; to seek the easy way and turn aside from suffering; to forget that the source of Christian life is to be found in the death and resurrection of Christ. Jesus redeemed humankind as the Suffering Servant and as Son of Man: by being one of us and in solidarity with his fellow men and women. We are redeemed by uniting ourselves with Christ. It is the way of countering the temptations that assail us.

PRAYER

There is no doubt at all that Jesus did pray; the gospels, and Hebrews, are explicit. Mark, with endearing candour, tells us that Jesus' addiction to prayer was something of a trial for his disciples. The evangelist has given a sample day in the early Galilean ministry, at Capernaum (Mk 1:21-34), a day of enthusiastic reception and of great promise. His disciples, caught up in the excitement, were chagrined when Jesus went missing (v 37) – 'In the morning, while it was still very dark, he got up and went out to a deserted place, and there he prayed.' Jesus had slept (he 'got up'), had snatched a few hours of sleep. For his mission he needed deeper refreshment, a more potent source of energy, and he found it in prayer to his Abba. His Abba was Sustainer of all. As one 'like us in every respect', Jesus was wholly dependent on this God. He turned, spontaneously, to an Abba who would support him, who would back him in his endeavours. True, he was sent, one who had to plough his own furrow. But he was not alone because the Father was with him. His prayer is graphic expression of his human dependence, of his human need.

The prayer of Jesus, by example, not by contrived design, is meant to alert disciples to their dependence on God. If the Son had found need and a joy in converse with his Father, he could expect that the other children of God, his sisters and brothers, would, too, experience that need and that happiness. The comforting fact is that Jesus, now as our high priest, has not ended his prayer. Returned to the Father, he has no need, any more, to pray for himself. As high priest he now prays for us, makes intercession for us, without respite (see Heb 7:25).

Vindicator of the Poor

Jesus had a free attitude to property. Himself of 'lower middle-class' Galilean background – he was a *tektón*, an artisan – he took for granted the owning of property. On the other hand, Jesus himself, during his itinerant mission, had no possessions. And he did, with severity, attack wealth where it had captured people's hearts and had blinded their eyes to God's purpose. He had especially in mind surplus wealth: the rich ought to use their wealth to benefit the poor. An aspect of the camel-saying – 'It is easier for a camel to go through the eye of a needle than for someone who is rich to enter the kingdom of God' (Mk 10:25, parr.) – is that it expresses the real difficulty the rich have in freeing themselves of possessiveness.

Jesus knew it to be his vocation to proclaim the true God – the Father. He knew that in faithfulness to his task he was making the kingdom present; in other words, he was proclaiming the coming of God as salvation for humankind. How he saw his task is vividly portrayed in Luke's introduction to Jesus' ministry (Lk 4:14-30). Coming to his Nazareth synagogue on a sabbath, Jesus was invited to take the scripture reading. He opened the scroll of Isaiah and read out:

> The Spirit of the Lord is upon me
> because he has anointed me to bring good news to the poor.
> He has sent me to proclaim release to the captives
> and recovery of sight to the blind,
> to let the oppressed go free,
> to proclaim the year of the Lord's favour.

He had taken care to close his reading before the next phrase of the Isaian passage – 'and the day of vengeance of our God' (Is 61:20). 'Vengeance' would be no part of his message. Then he declared: 'Today this scripture has been fulfilled in your hearing' (Lk 4:21). This Lucan Jesus displays a gracious concern for the 'little ones.' Instances leap to mind: the raising of a poor widow's son (7:11-17), welcome of the 'lost boy' (15:11-24), healing of a crippled woman (13:10-17). Most eloquent, perhaps, is Jesus' delicate response to the extravagant and brave gesture of the woman who had experienced his understanding and forgiving love (7:36-52).

WOMEN

Arguably, the most important text of the earliest Jesus tradition is the beatitude addressed to the poor: 'Blessed are the poor, for the kingdom is theirs' (see Lk 6:20). It is a fulfilment of Is 61:1 – 'He has sent me to bring good news to the oppressed' – a promise that the wretched lot of the poor will be reversed under the reign of God. The 'poor' are, surely, the economically poor. The term can carry a wider brief and include the marginalised. In the world of the day, women fell into that category. If his mission were 'good news to the poor', then Jesus' contact with women, still visible in the gospel tradition, must have been vastly more prevalent than our sources would seem to allow. Jesus' attitude towards women tells us much of his rich and sensitive humanity.

'The poor have the good news preached to them'. The poor include women, not only inevitably so in the nature of things, but also in view of the 'widow and orphan', the archetypal poor of biblical tradition. It surely must be perfectly obvious that 'poor' is an inclusive term. So, too, is the term 'disciple'! This is evident in Mark. The women ('Mary Magdalene, and Mary the mother of James the younger and of Joses, and Salome') who, standing at a distance, witnessed the crucifixion of Jesus, are described as those who 'followed him' – a technical term for discipleship. For that matter, the 'many other women' mentioned in the same context are also disciples (Mk 15:40-41). It is, of course, true that Luke speaks of these Galilean women only as those who 'provided for them out of their resources' (Lk 8:3). While that material provision may well have been welcome, failure to designate these women as disciples is tendentious. The fact remains: Jesus' disciples were men and women. Women, as well as men, went about with him. It should be helpful now to look at gospel passages where women do explicitly figure.

The Pagan Woman (Mk 7:24-30)
A woman who met Jesus was 'a Gentile, of Syrophoenician origin' – in other words, a Gentile by birth and religion. Her request for the healing of her daughter was refused because, as Jesus tells her, the rules did not allow it. His mission was to the chosen people: his 'bread' was not for 'dogs': a contemptuous Jewish label for Gentiles. She will not be put off: all very well indeed – but even the dogs get crumbs! And Jesus responded to the challenge.

The Anointing (Lk 14:3-9)
The woman is not named: interest falls on the saying (vv 7-9). She is

obviously a disciple – how else could one account for her gesture? She, however vaguely, has recognised him as Israel's Messiah. Jesus graciously accepted anointing – but related it to his death. The woman has made a lovely gesture, more meaningful than she knew; she, the woman-disciple, shows an understanding that the men-disciples lack (Mt 26:80). Her gracious deed will win her immortality: 'Truly I tell you, wherever the good news is proclaimed in the whole world, what she has done will be told in remembrance of her.' Here, surely, one cannot blame the gospel text: the deed of this woman is firmly highlighted. But what has happened to the story in Christian tradition? Has that 'beautiful thing' become a familiar part of the gospel knowledge of Christians?

> Wherever the gospel is proclaimed and the eucharist celebrated another story is told: the story of the apostle who betrayed Jesus. The name of the betrayer is remembered, but the name of the faithful disciple is forgotten because she was a woman.[6]

Has anyone got a better explanation?

Response to Forgiveness (7:36-50)

Nowhere more clearly than in Lk 7:36-50, the story of 'a woman in the city who was a sinner' (v 37), do we see a Jesus of delicate concern. The context, too, is admirable: here indeed is the 'friend of sinners' (v 34). Though 'sinner' is of wider connotation, the impression is that this woman was a prostitute and was well known as such (v 30). Luke has courteously refrained from naming her and she must remain anonymous. She was a woman who had previously encountered Jesus and had received his forgiveness. She had come back to thank him. She made a brave and extravagant gesture. She, a woman and a sinner to boot, dared to crash this 'stag party.' She kissed and anointed the feet of a reclining Jesus, to the evident scandal of his Pharisee host. Jesus, on the other hand, accepted her presence and ministry with gentle courtesy. And his verdict was clear and to the point: 'Her great love proves that her sins have been forgiven' (v 47).

Martha and Mary (Lk 10:38-42)

Important for appreciating Jesus' attitude towards women is his well-documented friendship with the sisters of Bethany. In John 11:1-44 Martha and Mary have the same contrasting temperaments as in Luke's narrative. The familiar relationship between Jesus and the women, explicitly remarked in Jn 11:5 – 'Jesus loved Martha and her sister' – is here graphically portrayed: an exasperated Martha does not hesitate to point out that it is Jesus' fault that she had been left on her own to make all the preparations (Lk 10:40). He gently chided her for her agitation. We find a parallel bluntness in Jn 11:21 when Martha complains: 'If you had been here, my brother would not have died.' Jesus and the sisters had, obviously, a mutually familiar friendship. He would surely have had other women friends. He had a healthy need of such friendship.

CHILDREN

Noteworthy is Jesus' respect for children. He proposed them as models of discipleship. In Mk 9:33-37 he countered the ambition of his disciples: 'Whoever wants to be first must be last of all and servant of all' and backed up his words with a prophetic gesture. He called to him a little child and, unconventionally, took the child in his arms. A revealing text is 10:13-16. Here I would quote from my book, *The Jesus Story*, where I have Jesus speak in the first person:

> I noticed that the disciples were involved in something of a hassle. I could hear indignant womens' voices. When I discovered what the matter was I, too, became indignant. Mothers had come with their little ones, looking for me to touch them – only that. The disciples were officiously 'protecting' me and demanding: 'get those brats out of here.' The mothers, bless them, were not so easily put off. They had sensed that I did not share the current disdain for children – and they were right. I sharply bade the disciples to let those women be and told them, bluntly, that these children were the ideal citizens of the kingdom. They, better than any other, are suited to the kingdom, for the kingdom is gift to be received with simplicity. And I added that no one could enter upon the blessing of the rule of God who is not open and willing to welcome it as gift. For that matter, since the rule was present in and through me, these little children had a privileged right of access to me. I called them and they ran to me. And I did what no adult man would do – at least not in

public – I took them into my arms, tousled their hair, and blessed them as they smiled and giggled. My men disciples looked on in glum discomfiture – how common! The mothers beamed their delight. Women are so much more perceptive. I was willing to wager that my women disciples would prove more constant than their brothers.[7]

FRIEND OF SINNERS

The parables of Luke 15 which deal with the reprieve of sinners are Jesus' answer to the 'scandal' of the Pharisees: 'All the tax collectors and sinners were coming to listen to him. And the Pharisees and the scribes were grumbling and saying, "This fellow welcomes sinners and eats with them".' (15:1-2). These parables reveal God's compassion for sinners, not as a timeless, general truth but as realised in the ministry of Jesus. The lost sheep is dearer to this Shepherd, this Jesus, precisely because it is lost! The parables demonstrate that the words and actions of Jesus are inseparable. He was not a teacher of morals outlining principles of conduct. Instead, his attitude towards, and his daily life with, the poor are the model of our behaviour. He has fulfilled perfectly – as he no doubt inspired – the words of counsel given later to his followers: 'Little children, let us love, not in word or speech, but in truth and action' (1 Jn 3:18).

If we are truly to appreciate the scandal of the righteous at Jesus' befriending of sinners, we must understand who the sinners are. The term 'sinners' in the Old Testament refers to people who, in some fundamental way, stand outside the Law. The Greek Bible rendered the Hebrew *reshaim*, 'wicked', by *hamartoloi* ('sinners') and Greek-speaking Jews used the term of the non-observant who had placed themselves outside the covenant. The 'sinners' of the gospels are these 'wicked' people regarded as living blatantly outside the Law. Jesus counted such within his fellowship. This was conduct that genuinely caused serious offence.

Jesus had tablefellowship with sinners. He, in a manner that they could understand, assured them that God loved them. Doubtless, he hoped that they would change their ways, but he did not threaten. One thinks, for instance, of Zacchaeus in his sycamore tree. A preacher of repentance might have read the riot act to a spectacularly captive hearer. Instead, Jesus casually invited himself to dinner in his home. A sermon would have left him unmoved – he had been too often preached at. The novel approach changed his life (Lk 19:1-10).

The stories of the woman sinner and of Zacchaeus show that Jesus was not in the business of saving 'souls'; he was concerned with people. Jesus was friend of sinners – he brought hope into their lives. As 'image of the invisible God' he imaged the *Deus humanissimus* – the God bent on the salvation of humankind. We move, now, to an area where the human vulnerability of Jesus is most in evidence.

SUFFERING AND DEATH

Our human history, before the *eschaton* (the End), is one largely compounded of suffering. It is therefore 'fitting' (Heb 2:10), in accordance with the character of our God, that in seeking to bring humankind to 'glory', the destined End, in and through Jesus, he should have Jesus walk the road of suffering. He has become *one of us*, sharing our sorrow and our anxiety, in order to be the first to reach perfection – the first to become *the true image* of God, the first to become *wholly human*. It is fitting that, trapped in a history of suffering, we should be set free by one who has entered into that suffering and made it his own (2:10). We can truly see God in the face of Jesus.

For the author of Hebrews, Jesus is Son of God; but he is, as we have noted, the Son who 'had to become like his brothers and sisters in every respect' (2:17). He is the human being who stands in a relationship of obedient faithfulness towards God (3:16) and who stands in solidarity with human suffering. Thus he is mediator: a true priest who can bring humankind to God. If he bears 'the exact imprint of God's very being' (1:3), it is because we see in him what makes God God; he shows us that God is God of humankind.

Gethsemane (14:32-42)

Mark's gospel is a theology of the cross. Understandably, this concern comes to a head in his passion narrative. It is evident in the Gethsemane episode (14:32-44) – 'he began to be distressed and agitated' (v 33): Jesus is shattered. He died with an anguished shout:

'My God, my God, why have you forsaken me?' (15:34). Mark has Jesus die in total isolation, without any relieving feature at all. It is only after death that Jesus is clearly recognised and acknowledged by any human in the awed confession of the centurion: 'Truly, this man was God's Son!' (15:39). Mark is making a theological point: salvation is never of oneself, not even for Jesus. That awful journey to the cross is comfort for all who have seen in Jesus of Nazareth the image of the invisible God. It is the consolation of all who have found in him the ultimate assurance that God is on our side. It is, above all, comfort to all who find it hard to bear the cross. It was not easy for the Master.

Godforsakenness (Mk 15:14)

Jesus suffered the absence of God. His cry of dereliction was one of total desolation: 'My God, my God, why have you forsaken me?' His words are the opening of Psalm 22 – a lament. Lament is the cry of a suffering righteous person addressed to the One who can bring an end to suffering. It would have seemed that, up to this point, Jesus' isolation could go no further: deserted by his disciples, taunted by his enemies, derided by those who hung with him, suffocating in the darkness of evil. But the worst was now: abandoned by God. His suffering was radically lonely. But this God was 'my God' (v 34). Even in this, as at Gethsemane, it was 'not what I want, but what you want.' Here, even more than then, the sheer humanness of Jesus was manifest. What one discovers here is the difference between feeling and reality. Jesus felt abandoned. The reality was: never were Father and Son more closely one. It is the experience of a Job who shouts out at a silent God. It is the mystical experience of the dark night of the soul. At that moment, Jesus had an over-whelming sense of failure.

Failure?

The truth of the matter is that his death marked Jesus as historically a failure. Jesus was executed on the order of a Roman provincial official: an alleged trouble-maker in that bothersome province of Judaea had been summarily dealt with. The incident did not raise a ripple in imperial affairs. Yet history has shown that this execution was an event of historic proportions. Its ripples flow stronger than ever two thousand years later.

Let us be clear about it. The Romans and the Jewish Sanhedrin had effectively closed the 'Jesus case'. The aims and message of Jesus had ended with his death. His prophetic voice had been muzzled. This is failure. The question: Why had Jesus been silenced? It was because he, unflinchingly, had lived and preached God's love for humankind. That is why he had tablefellowship with sinners, why he sought to free women and men from the tyranny of religion, why he, at every hand's turn, bore witness to the true God. He might, in face of the threatening opposition, have packed it in and gone home to Nazareth. That would have been failure indeed. But he would not be turned from witnessing to God's love. They might take his life, but to his last breath he would witness. What Jesus tells us is that failure is not the last word. That is, as God views failure.

The crucial question is: did Jesus see and experience crucifixion as the failure of his plans? I believe that the answer is: yes. Of course, one must be clear as to what his plan was. We should realise that Jesus did not come to establish a new Israel. His call was to *metanoia*, to a radical change of heart; he had come to *renew* Israel. A surely authentic word of Jesus (because it must have been embarrassing for a church that had turned to the Gentiles) is the declaration: 'I was sent only to the lost sheep of the house of Israel' (Mt 15:24; see 10:6). He had come to summon Israel to become what God wanted his people to be. His life had been spent in that task. Now, popular disillusionment and official rejection had frustrated that task; sentence of death had brought it to a jarring halt. He can no longer preach the rule of God. Though he was in no way responsible for it, and had done everything to avoid failure, he was draining the bitter dregs of failure. There, I believe, is another dimension of the anguished cry: 'My God, my God, why have you forsaken me?'

Jesus came to bear witness to a God bent on humankind. Now he entrusts his experience of failure to God. He, like us, had to reconcile a painful experience of failure with trust in God. The synoptists, and especially Mark, show that in no way did Jesus begin his mission with a vision of violent death at the end of the road. And if at a later stage he had to face the fact that violent death was the likely outcome, the Gethsemane episode shows that, though he still did not fully understand God's way, he filially bowed to the Father's will. His Gethsemane decision was to trust in God despite the darkness of his situation. This was his most severe testing.

Jesus of Nazareth was a first-century Galilean Jew, a village carpenter. He was in his thirties when he encountered the prophet John the Baptist and became John's disciple. This was the first of several major decisions. He could sin. In practice, to the end, he always took the right and moral choice. His trustful prayer underlined his dependence on the Father and, surely, helped him, mightily, in his consistent pursuit of the right and better way.

In his own mission, he bore unfailing witness to a loving, gracious Father. Consequently, he was extremely sensitive to the needy, the suffering. He had a preferential option for the poor and the outcast. Indeed, he had won notoriety as friend of sinners. As a healthy, sexually mature man, he had an easy rapport with women, whom he treated with unfailing courtesy. He had, unusually for his day, a profound respect for children.

Jesus entered, fully, into our human lot of suffering and death. It is, surely, comfort that he needed assurance of God's purpose for him. It is comfort that he feared the prospect of an atrocious death. He had a painful feeling of failure: the bottom had fallen out of his world. He cried out, in consternation, to his God. In reality, this failure was his triumph. He was experiencing what Paul was to perceive: the scandal of the cross. The scandal is the infinite reach of the love of God:

> If God is for us, who is against us? He who did not withhold his own Son, but gave him up for all of us, will he not with him also give us everything else? (Rom 8:32).

CHAPTER 3

Introduction: Infancy Narrative

She will bear a son, and you are to name him Jesus,
for he will save his people from their sins. (Mt 1:21)

THE GENEALOGY OF JESUS (Mt 1:1-17)

The Old Testament, especially Genesis and 1 Chronicles, makes skillful use of genealogies. In his turn, Matthew finds his genealogy to be an effective way of establishing the identity of Jesus. He traces Jesus' ancestry back to David and Abraham: 'An account of the genealogy of Jesus the Messiah, the son of David, the son of Abraham' (1:1). In particular, he shows that the one whom Christians proclaim as 'Messiah' can be correctly named 'son of David'.

Matthew's pattern of three sets of 14 generations is patently artificial; to get his 'fourteen generations from David to the Exile' he passed over in silence some of the kings of Judah. He appears to have been influenced by current apocalyptic thought which cast world history in periods of seven, in other words, 'weeks' of years. For Israel's history Matthew counts 'two "weeks" of generations (2 x 7 = 14 generations), from Israel's beginnings in Abraham to its high point in *King* David, two more weeks from its high point to its low point in the disaster of the Babylonian exile, and two further weeks during its ascent to its goal, Jesus the Messiah. Jesus Christ thus begins the seventh period, the period of perfection and fulfilment (see Daniel's seventy weeks of years in Dan 9). Hence Matthew uses an apocalyptic convention to proclaim that God has secretly ordered the economy of salvation so that all of Israel's history moves smoothly towards the Messiah.'8

One must note that this Jesus is not only son of David – he is also

31

'the son of Abraham.' As such he is fulfilment of the promise that
through Abraham 'all the nations of the earth' would be blessed
(Gen 12:3; 22:18). Significantly, the gospel closes with the commission to 'make disciples of all nations' (Mt 28:19). With his designation of Jesus as 'the son of David, the son of Abraham', Matthew is
declaring the Messiah to be the Saviour (1:21) of Jew and Gentile.

When one looks at Matthew's list, one finds a mixed bag. To an
extent we are faced with names only. But we can put faces on a
goodly number of the names – and not all are prepossessing. Jesus'
ancestry is not a saintly line; it is, in generous measure, disrep-
utable. True, it begins on a high note, with Abraham the man of
faith – who is followed by a weak Isaac and a rascally Jacob. It is
comforting to stress this aspect of the genealogy. One might say
that Matthew is, in his manner, making the same point as the
author of Hebrews: the sinless Jesus is 'like his brothers and sisters
in every respect' (Heb 2:17). He had no control over his ancestry.
There is, too, the comforting assurance that God 'can write straight
on crooked lines,' that inadequate humans cannot thwart his purpose. They may indeed serve his purpose.

THE WOMEN

A fascinating feature of Matthew's genealogy is the prominence of
women in his list. One would have expected Mary, of course, but
not the others: Tamar, Rahab, Ruth, Bathsheba. Their presence is
due to the fact that they are 'holy irregularities': there is something
not quite regular in the relationship of each with her spouse. Tamar
(Gen 38) is an obvious example. She had been married to Er, son of
Judah, who died without issue. According to levirate law (Deut
25:5-6), it was the duty of the next son, Onan, to marry the widow;
the first son of that union would be regarded as son of the deceased,
so guaranteeing the only immortality he might have.[9]

Tamar had been hard done by her father-in-law who would
deprive her of her legal right. Her claim was not selfish: she was
upholding the cause of her dead husband. She took the law into her
own hands. In the event, Judah has to admit: 'She is more righteous
than I' (Gen 38:26). To see in Tamar's conduct an example of the end

justifying the means is, for us, an obvious temptation – and a glaring instance of missing the point of biblical story. It is obvious that, in its context, her conduct is admirable: she was a woman of her day and age. She has done no more than the exploited widow of Jesus' parable: she had, in the face of male callousness, taken a womanly way to get her way (see Lk 18:2-5). A message is that the little ones of this world, the marginalised, have a God-given right to vindicate their rights. Is it not, after all, the message of the *Magnificat?*

Rahab and Ruth are less easy to assess. In the genealogy Rahab appears as wife of Salmon and mother of Boaz. She is certainly the Rahab of Joshua 2 – she who had sheltered Joshua's spies. A snag is that Boaz comes nearly two centuries later than the age of Joshua; a marriage of Rahab and Salmon is unlikely, to put it mildly! Straightway, for us, a problem. Biblical writers would shrug and ask: 'What problem?' They put their question, not ours. Rahab was a woman who had read the writing on the wall. Jericho was doomed – she cut her losses and threw in her lot with the eventual conquerors. Not very noble, perhaps, but surely very human.

Ruth, a Moabitess, having lost her Israelite husband, elected to stick with her mother-in-law, Naomi. The shrewd older woman was able to engineer a marriage for Ruth with Boaz, kinsman of her late husband. There is more than a suggestion that he was cleverly manipulated by the women. But all turned out well. Ruth, the Moabitess, became great-grandmother of David. Ruth is a touching human story. As in the case of Tamar there is concern for the right of a dead husband. There is, in Naomi and Ruth, an edifying love bond between mother-in-law and daughter-in-law. And there is the charming touch: two admirable women do, gently, manipulate an admirable man.

Bathsheba –'the wife of Uriah' – is rather different (2 Sam 11). It is easy enough to see that she was not notably upset at having caught the attention of King David. And there is no evidence of overwhelming grief at the death of her husband. Indeed, her major role in winning the throne for her son Solomon, and his obvious acknowledgement of her part, make clear that she was an ambitious woman. She is, in my view, the least attractive of the four.

There we have them. Now, what of us? We can ask ourselves if we have anything like Tamar's passion for justice. Rahab might alert us to a temptation to cut our losses. True, she had ended up on the winning side – but could she really live with herself? The love of the older and the younger women, Naomi and Ruth, of different nationalities, is surely a headline. And there is the message that romance, and a dash of female charm, are precious human values. We should be grateful that we have the gift of the Song of Songs, that celebration of sexual love. There is the less savoury but no less human side. The love-affair of David and Bathsheba led to the callous murder of an innocent Uriah. We are joyously reminded that human love, when it is truly such, is God's loveliest gift to humankind. We are painfully reminded that we humans can pervert love. It seems to me that the four women are, in diverse ways, a radical challenge to us. They are a challenge to what can be best and what might be worst in our humanness.

CONCLUSION

Matthew's genealogy has told the reader that Jesus is 'son of David' and 'son of Abraham.' Matthew leaves the 'son of Abraham' motif and its Gentile connotation until the story of the Magi (Mt 2:1-12) and concentrates first on son of David. What emerges is that Jesus is of the Messianic line. What we have been at pains to show is that he is of *this* line. Here is documentation to back up the assertion in Hebrews that he is like us in all things. Jesus of Nazareth is of the human family of David. Jesus the Saviour is of the human race. There is our comfort and our hope.

THE INFANCY NARRATIVE (MT 1:18-2:23)

The Infancy Narratives of Matthew and Luke have had a notable influence on Christian tradition and have put a profound mark on Christian art. The long Christian appreciation of them has not been misplaced. We had sensed that there was something special here – that these texts said quite a lot more than they appeared to say. In our day we have, happily, come to realise that both infancy narratives – which are wholly independent of each other – are, first and foremost, christological statements. It is along this line, and only here, that we can grasp their true meaning.[10]

Matthew 1-2

Matthew and Luke shared a twofold tradition: Jesus' home was Nazareth; Jesus was descendant of David and, as such, appropriately born in Bethlehem. Reconciliation of these traditions has influenced the shape of their narratives. For Matthew, Jesus' birth in Bethlehem offered no problem; in his view, Bethlehem was home of Joseph and Mary. He has to move Jesus from Bethlehem to Nazareth. For Luke, on the other hand, the home of Joseph and Mary was Nazareth. He has to arrange to have Jesus born in Bethlehem. This contrived reconciliation, by each evangelist, of the dominant Nazareth tradition (throughout the gospels Jesus is counted a Nazarene) with the Bethlehem tradition, would suggest that birth at Bethlehem is to be taken as a theologoumenon (a theological affirmation related as an historical event) – in this case an affirmation of the Davidic descent of Jesus.

In building his infancy narrative Matthew has made use of two main blocks of material: a cycle of angelic dream appearances, and the Magi story. The material has been thoroughly edited by Matthew but the two blocks are still recognisably distinct. Angelic dream appearances: 1:20-25; 2:13-15; 2:19-23. It is evident that Joseph wears the cloak of the famous patriarch Joseph, especially in his being a man of dreams and in his going down to Egypt. The Magi story: 2:1-12. As it stands, this is a self-contained story, with no mention of Joseph. Matthew composed its sequel (2:16-18) when he combined it with the flight into Egypt episode.

A feature of Matthew's gospel is his use of formula citations (Old Testament quotations) which sit loosely in their context. They are notably frequent in his infancy narrative: 1:22-23; 2:5-6; 2:15; 2:17-18; 2:23. Matthew has recognised the applicability of particular Old Testament texts to particular incidents in Jesus' career. He introduced them because they fit his theology of the oneness of God's plan and because they help to bring out, for his Christian readers, who and what Jesus is. Thus, the five infancy narrative citations tell us that the virginally-conceived Jesus is God-with-us, that as Son of David he was, fittingly, born in Bethlehem, that, in being called out of Egypt, he re-enacted the Exodus of his people, that he suffered the Exile of his people, and that as the Nazorean he began his saving work.

The Birth of Jesus

Joseph and Mary were betrothed. In Jewish society, betrothal was something far more more serious than our marriage engagement. Betrothal was really a marriage contract, except that the partners had not begun to live together. Joseph discovered that his betrothed was pregnant 'of the Holy Spirit' is Matthew's nod to the reader; Joseph was not aware of that factor and was in a quandary. He was a 'righteous' man, that is, Law-observant. He assumed that Mary had been unfaithful. The death penalty for adultery (Deut 22:23-27) was not then, if ever it had been, in force; divorce was the answer. This was the course Joseph decided on – except that he wanted to divorce her 'quietly.' It is not clear how he could have hoped to achieve this. And divorce would not have helped Mary at all. She would have been left on her own to bear her baby – in a thoroughly disapproving society. The 'righteous' man, Joseph, was a confused man. He desperately wanted to do the decent thing, but his 'solution' was no solution at all.

Happily for him – and for Mary – God took a hand. In a dream all was made clear. Mary was not an unfaithful bride but a wholly privileged instrument of God. Her child, of divine parenthood, would be Saviour; he is the one who 'will save his people for their sins.' And here Matthew throws in his formula-citation. He looked to Is 7:14 (in the Greek) and found there a word of promise: 'the virgin would bear a son'. That son will be Emmanuel, God-with-us. Cleverly, Matthew has anticipated the close of his gospel: 'Remember, I am with you always' (Mt 28:20). In that unique child of Mary, a first-century Palestinian Jew, we meet our God. Paul had put it in his inimitable fashion: 'God was in Christ, reconciling the world to himself' (2 Cor 5:19).

The Magi Story (2:1-12).

In this narrative, Matthew has cast back into the infancy the reactions that, historically, greeted the proclamation of the risen Lord: some believed and paid homage; others rejected the message and the preachers. In other words, christological revelation was followed by proclamation and by the twofold reaction of acceptance/homage and rejection/persecution. But this had been prepared for in the ministry of Jesus. The same pattern is presented in the infancy narrative.

There seems little point in looking for the homeland of the Magi – whom Matthew seemingly regards as astrologers of some sort. Nor is there any point in looking to a comet, a supernova, or a planetary conjunction to account for 'his star' (1:2). A star which rises, goes before, and comes to rest over a place is no natural phenomenon but a miraculous (more precisely, a symbolic) star. More to the point is that, for Matthew, the Magi represent the Gentiles, fittingly alerted not by an angel (as Luke's Jewish shepherds) but by a star. The liturgical tradition of the feast of Epiphany has caught Matthew's intent. The Magis' role as prefiguring the acceptance of Gentiles into the Christian community points toward the universal character of the gospel. Jesus is functioning as son of Abraham.

The Balaam narrative of Numbers 22-24, embroidered with Jewish tradition, would, skillfully used by Matthew, appear to have been the inspiration of the Magi story. Balaam was summoned by Balak 'from the east' to curse Israel. Significantly, Philo calls him a *magos*. Similarly, Herod tried to use the Magi for his own ends. In his oracle Balaam had declared: 'A star shall come out of Jacob, and a sceptre shall rise out of Israel' (Num 24:17). Here, credibly, is 'his star' (Mt 2:2).

Flight and Return (2:13-23)

The next two episodes are coloured by the story of Moses in Egypt – again as elaborated in Jewish tradition – and also echo the Exodus motif. The basic story line in 2:13-15 concerns the rescue of the child saviour from the machinations of the wicked king by flight into Egypt. Jewish tradition, as we find it, for example, in Josephus, had it that the Pharaoh of the Exodus had been forewarned by one of his 'sacred scribes' of the birth of a Hebrew who would constitute a threat to the Egyptian kingdom. Pharaoh and the whole of Egypt were filled with dread (see Mt 2:3). Pharaoh's plan was frustrated by a warning communicated in a dream to Moses' father. The parallels between this Jewish legend and the pre-Matthean infancy narrative are manifest. Read against the background of Exodus 1-2 Jesus emerges as a Moses-figure. The Hosea quotation – 'Out of Egypt have I called my son' – refers to the exodus of Israel from Egypt. Matthew sees that Jesus relives the history of his people, not only in the Exile but in the previous going down into Egypt.

The story line in 2:16-18, involving the massacre of the male children in Bethlehem, echoes Pharaoh's decree against the male infants of the Hebrews. Matthew, with his formula citation of Jeremiah 31:15, works in another theme: that of the Babylonian Exile. Again, Jesus is associated with a tragic event of his people. The names in the three formula citations: Bethlehem (the city of David), Egypt (the land of the Exodus) and Ramah (the mourning place of the Exile) are theologically suggestive. The final episode (2:19-23), too, gives us three significant names: Israel, Galilee and Nazareth. The 'citation' here is not really such: Matthew is playing on the name Nazareth. Quite likely, he is thinking of the *neser*, 'branch' of Is 11:1 and of *nazir* – one consecrated to God. At any rate he knows that this son of David, Son of God, is none other than Jesus the Nazorean.

In the following chapters we look at this 'Nazorean' through Matthew's eyes. I have, previously, striven to discern the distinctive christological insights of Mark and Luke. Now I add the view of Matthew. I find refreshing pluralism. And that before throwing in the heady brew of Paul and John.

CHAPTER 4

Proclamation of the Kingdom

Everyone who hears these words of mine and acts on them
will be like a wise man who built his house on rock (Mt 7:24).

PRELIMINARY MANIFESTATIONS 3-4

A summary of the preaching of John the Baptist (Mt 3:1- 12) leads to the baptism of Jesus (3:13-17). In Matthew's account the emphasis is on the revelation of Jesus as Son of God, not on the baptism as such. Jesus came to be baptised. Why? To inaugurate his mission (and, in effect, the messianic era); to raise the baptism of John to a new level; to show his solidarity with sinful humankind; to give an example of humility. The vision (3:16) sets the seal of divine approval on this mission of Jesus.

Here only in the Synoptic accounts of the baptism does the Baptist recognise Jesus before the baptism. He tries to prevent Jesus from undergoing this baptism of repentance meant for sinners. Jesus appeals to God's plan of salvation. It befits John and him 'to fulfil all righteousness', to conform to the roles mapped out for them. Matthew's text shows the Christian embarrassment (quite absent from Mk 1:9) that Jesus should have undergone a 'baptism of repentance for the forgiveness of sins' (see Mk 1:4) and at the hands of his inferior, John. The voice of the Father is for all present (and not for Jesus alone as in Mark): Jesus is not being designated Son for the first time ('You are my beloved son' – Mark). Rather, his sonship is proclaimed to others: 'This is my beloved Son.'

The Testing (4:1-11)

Each gospel shows Jesus subjected to temptation, to testing. Even John, who does not mention the forty days in the desert, shows moments in the public ministry when Jesus' fidelity came under pressure. The letter to the Hebrews is emphatic that Jesus was tested in all things as we are, yet without sinning (Heb 4:15). Our Synoptic wilderness accounts are expressing in stylised form the broadly based New Testament conviction that Jesus had to struggle to remain faithful to God's will.

At the start of this passage, Matthew shows Jesus experiencing what Israel had experienced in the desert – with the radical difference that this Son will conquer where God's son Israel had failed (Deut 8:2-5). The tempter immediately latches on to the question of Jesus' sonship. (It ought to be obvious that a literalist interpretation – and, a fortiori, presentation – of the 'temptations' must be avoided. This is a sophisticated piece of writing and one must correctly grasp Matthew's intent). At the baptism Jesus had been solemnly acclaimed as God's Son (3:17); the question now is: how will he *function* as God's Son? One should have in mind that Matthew is addressing his *Christian* community. In terms of this 'temptation' of the Lord he is reading them a salutary lesson.

Jesus will not misuse his sonship to his own advantage (first temptation); his disciple will not abuse his or her christian status. In quoting Deut 8:3 Jesus had urged his trust in God; now he is challenged to turn that trust into crass presumption (second temptation); the true Christian will not seek to put God to the test. Building on the promise that the Messiah-Son would have the nations for his inheritance (Ps 2:6-8), the 'ruler of this world' (Jn 12:31; 16:11) presents himself as a god to be worshipped – only to be unceremoniously repudiated. This bizarre episode is readily understandable when we recall the basic temptation of Israel to idolatry and when we observe that Jesus' reply is an emphatic assertion of God's fundamental command to Israel: monotheism (Deut 6:13). The Christian will, likewise, reject any form of idolatry – the idolatry of wealth, of ambition...

Proclamation and Call (4:17-22)

Matthew situates Jesus' public ministry just after John had been arrested ('delivered up', anticipating the delivering up of Jesus to his passion). Jesus' preaching, 'Repent, for the kingdom of heaven has come near', continues the Baptist's call to conversion. He catches up the torch from the hand of John.

Jesus summoned his hearers to repent (change their lives) because they had not allowed the rule of God to become effective in their lives. The expression 'kingdom of heaven' is rich in meaning. It signifies God's rule on earth, his reign in people's hearts. It means the fulfilment of the promises, the fullness of blessings, in short, the new order of things to come, an order already present in the person of Jesus. What Jesus claimed was that the decisive intervention of God was happening in his ministry: God is acting in and through the ministry of Jesus and his disciples. The kingdom is here and now present in history in that the power of evil spirits is broken, sins are forgiven, sinners are gathered into Jesus' friendship. These events are present to human experience, and they are so whether people are aware of them or not. The kingdom comes as a present offer, in actual gift, through the proclamation of the gospel. But it only fully arrives on condition of the positive response of the hearer.

The proclamation of the kingdom of heaven and the call to conversion were personalised by Jesus' inviting of Peter, Andrew, James and John to discipleship. The evangelist's description of the call is more interested in the theological aspect than in the facts. (Jn 1:35-42 has quite a different account). When Jesus called all four answered 'immediately', leaving their nets (symbol of their former way of life) behind them. The creative word, meeting them in their everyday world, laid hold of them and changed their lives forever. This call of the first disciples became the model for all calls to discipleship in the church.

THE SERMON ON THE MOUNT (Mt 5-7)

The Sermon on the Mount is the first of Matthew's five discourses. The setting (5:1) and the conclusion (7:28-29) indicate that, in his plan, the Sermon was addressed to all Israel gathered to hear Jesus. The basic theme is that Jesus came not to abolish the law and the Prophets but to fulfil them (5:17). Matthew had Jews in mind. More immediately, he has Jesus present what Christians must accept as his authoritative interpretation of the Torah.

Plan of the Sermon

Introduction 5:1-20
The Antitheses 5:21-24

Three Acts of Piety 6:1-18
Other Teachings 6:19-7:12
Warnings 7:13-29.

INTRODUCTION 5:1-20

Beatitudes (5:1-12)

Our gospels have two, notably different, versions of the beatitudes: Mt 5:3-12 and Lk 6:20-23. Matthew has nine beatitudes – where Luke has four, with four corresponding 'woes' (Lk 6:24-26). Matthew's beatitudes, as a whole, carry distinctive features. The expression 'poor in spirit' points to a transformation of the idea of 'the poor' – the literally poor (Lk 6:20). In current usage the designation 'poor in spirit' applies to one who is detached from worldly goods, who is interiorly free in regard to money. In fact it is frequently related to the possession of wealth: it is possible for an economically rich person to be 'poor in spirit'. This is because we take 'poor' in a specific sense, an economic sense, which may not be the biblical meaning. And that meaning, we now know from the Jewish texts of Qumran is 'humility'; the poor in spirit are the humble. The parallel beatitude of 'the meek' confirms this meaning. These beatitudes, in Matthew, are no longer addressed to those who lack the necessities of life (Luke/Jesus) but to those characterised by their meekness, their patience, their humility. They are the *anawim* with Jesus himself as the ultimate 'poor man' (11:29). It is evident that 'blessed are those who hunger and thirst for righteousness' is very different from Luke's blessedness of the 'poor' and the 'hungry'. For Matthew, Christianity has broadened and deepened the meaning of the term righteousness (5:20).

'Blessed are the pure in heart for they shall see God' (5:8). The qualification 'in heart' like 'in spirit' points to an interior disposition. What is in question is what we would call 'purity of intention', demanding perfect correspondence between intention and action. 'Pure in heart' characterises people of integrity. The beatitudes of the merciful and the peacemakers are concerned with action: the conduct of a Christian towards a neighbour who stands in need. The best illustration of 'merciful' is Matthew's description of the last judgment: 'I was hungry and you gave me food' (25:35-40). As for the 'peacemakers': these evoke a good work highly prized in Judaism. It was observed that, among those who needed help, the most needy were an estranged husband and wife or friends who have fallen out. To seek to reconcile them, to restore them to peace, is one of the kindest services one can render to the neighbour.

Where Luke applied the beatitudes to Christians as a suffering minority, Matthew has introduced a distinction: he reserves the blessedness promised in the beatitudes to Christians who truly live the gospel ideal. He had re-read the beatitudes in light of his pastoral preoccupation and had filled them out. He takes care to remind Christians that the promises of salvation are conditional ((5:2). We will not be admitted to the Kingdom unless, after the example of the Master, we have shown ourselves to be meek and humble; unless we have given proof of righteousness and loyalty; unless we have carried out what God has asked of us, in particular, unless we have served our brothers and sisters in their need.

> The Beatitudes are thoroughly Jewish in form and content. They challenged those who made up 'Israel' in Matthew's time by delineating the kinds of persons and actions that will receive their full reward when God's kingdom comes. They remind Christians today of the Jewish roots of their piety and challenge each generation to reflect on what persons and actions they consider to be important or 'blessed.'[11]

The Principle (5:17-20)

'Do not think that I have come to abolish the law or the prophets; I have come not to abolish but to fulfil' (5:17). The opening passage (5:17-20) sets the tone as it states the relation of the Mosaic Law to Jesus. Jesus had not come to destroy 'the law and the prophets': his mission is one of prophetic fulfilment. Nor did he come to *obey* the Law. He transcends it so that he, not the Law, is norm for the Christian. This is borne out by v 18 – 'until all is accomplished' refers to the event of the death-resurrection of Jesus. Post-Easter Christians will live by the 'law' of Jesus (7:24). Nevertheless, the Christian teacher will be faithful to the Law – as reinterpreted by Jesus (v 19). Christians are not to become better 'Pharisees'; they should not grow into legalists. Christianity is meant to have broadened and deepened the meaning of the term 'righteousness', the doing of God's will, according to the teaching of Jesus.

The Antitheses (5:21-48)

The principle of vv 17-20 is applied in the 'antitheses' (5:21-48). Six times, with a similar formula each time, the Law is quoted ('you have heard that it was said') to be followed by an 'antithetical' word of Jesus which modifies it ('but I say to you'). In the cases of murder, adultery and love Jesus radicalised the Law by extension and internalisation; in the cases of divorce, oaths and retaliation he abrogated the letter of the Law.

The first antithesis (vv 21-26) declares that anger is as a grave a crime as murder. Jesus interprets the fifth commandment so that it embraces all those feelings and emotions of which murder is the outcome. He moves to a strong recommendation of brotherly/sisterly reconciliation and warns that an unforgiving spirit will come between us and the God we would worship. In the second antithesis (vv 27-30) we are warned that adultery, too, is born in the heart. The sixth commandment, as reinterpreted by Jesus, reaches to all thoughts and desires that lead to sexual sin. One must have firmly in mind that Jesus, as a Jew, had a positive and healthy approach to human sexuality. There is no trace, in his teaching, of the neurosis that was to mark, so sadly, a prevalent strain in Christian attitudes to sexuality.

In the third antithesis (vv 31-32) Jesus revokes the Law's sanctioning of divorce (see Deut 24:1-4). Puzzling is the qualification 'except on the ground of unchastity.' It now seems reasonable to hold (evidence from the Qumran documents has helped) that by 'unchastity' (porneia) Matthew means marriages within prohibited degrees of consanguinity and affinity – 'incestuous' marriages. There is no question of divorce in such cases because there is no marriage to begin with. Jesus forbade divorce without qualification. The fourth antithesis (vv 33-37) is a radical rejection of a respected institution of the Torah: oaths and vows. The Matthean Jesus categorically declares: 'Do not swear at all' There is no way of reconciling this absolute prohibition with later church practice (recall the obligation of the anti-modernistic oath). And, to this day, the demand of a somewhat modified oath. Surely, that should make us think.

Too often the law of *talion*, 'an eye for an eye and a tooth for a tooth' is cited as an instance of primitive savagery. On the contrary it is an enlightened law designed to regulate and moderate retaliation – to 'make the punishment fit the crime' in short (see Ex 21:24; Lev 24:20; Deut 19:21). Here, again, Jesus revokes the letter of the Torah. *Not* 'a tooth for a tooth', careful correspondence of injury and compensation, but radical repudiation of any retaliation – 'turn the other cheek also'. G. B. Caird's illuminating comment on Revelation 13:10 ('Whoever is for captivity, to captivity he goes; whoever is to be slain by the sword, by the sword must he be slain.') opens up a wider perspective:

> When one man wrongs another, the other may retaliate, bear a grudge, or take his injury out on a third person. Whichever he does, there are now two evils where before there was one; and a chain reaction is started, like the spreading of a contagion. Only if the victim absorbs the wrong and so puts it out of currency, can it be prevented from going any further. And this is why the great ordeal is also the great victory.[12]

Jesus rules out all means, even legal action, of obtaining compensation. Strong stuff, indeed.

Despite the formulation of v 43, nowhere in the Law does it state that the Israelite should hate the enemy. We are faced with a popular modification of the love-command: the enemy of the just person or of God's people is an enemy of God. Besides, 'neighbour' would have been restricted to fellow-Jews and, consequently, there is no obligation to love the 'non- neighbour'. Jesus enlarged the range of 'neighbour' to apply to all without distinction of race (see Lk 10:29-37). He is not taking a sentimental or naive view that all people are, in practice, brothers and sisters. He maintains the category of enemy. If he demands love of enemies it is because the Father loves those whom we would count as his enemies. Unless they can display this all-embracing love, Christians are no better than others; they have not really experienced the love of their Father. Matthew speaks of perfection – meaning generous, single-hearted devotion to God and humankind. This is why to be perfect is the obligation of every Christian, or, at very least, our abiding challenge.

These demands, throughout the antitheses, are not intended as reg-
ulations for the conduct of daily life. But they are meant to be taken
seriously. They are vivid and even startling illustrations of the manner in which the quality and direction of God's treatment of his
children might be reproduced in human relationships. Jesus was
wholly aware of how much he asked of human nature when he sub-
stituted 'love your enemies' for 'love your neighbour.'

THREE ACTS OF PIETY 6:1-18

Almsgiving, prayer and fasting were traditional Jewish practices. In
each case it is question of a private act of piety. Admirable, when
performed simply, by sincere people. 'Hypocrites' can make an
unholy show of these good ways. Like chapter 23, the passage 6:1-
18 is an attack on the Jewish opponents of Matthew's community.
In chapter 23 the 'hypocrites' say but do not do; here what they do
is for show. Public displays of private piety are not for Jesus' followers.

One can readily see that, originally, the passage was made up of the
three units 6:2-4, 5-6, 16-18 – the uniform construction of the units
makes that much clear. It is obvious that Matthew took advantage
of the reference to prayer here to fill out the teaching of Jesus on the
subject (6:7-15).

'And when you pray, you must not be like the hypocrites' (6:5).
While the 'hypocrites' are the Jewish opponents, they also represent
a legalistic element within Matthew's community. 'When you are
praying': it is assumed that Christians will pray. What is in question
is how they ought to pray – or, in the first instance, how they ought
not pray. They must not make a spectacle of prayer. In vv 7-8 there
is another negative precept, but this time in view of Gentile practice. Invocation of pagan deities was regularly a fulsome affair. The
gods' attention had to be attracted, hence a prelude of elaborate
titles and adulatory attributes. There is no need for any of this when
one turns, trustfully, to an Abba – look at the Psalms. These negative rulings had cleared the way for the positive teaching of the
Lord: 'Pray then in this way' (6:9).

The Lord's Prayer 6:9-13

Matthew (6:9-13) and Luke (11:2-4) have given two versions of the Lord's Prayer. The first, obvious, difference is that Matthew's form is the longer. More importantly, Matthew has preserved the original strongly eschatological flavour of it, while Luke has adapted it to fit the modest pattern of day-by-day Christian living. Besides, the Matthean version is notably Jewish in tone, clearly congenial to Jewish Christians.

The first three petitions (vv 9-10) really boil down to the central one: 'Your kingdom come.' The disciples pray that God will show forth his saving will by bringing about his definitive Rule over humankind. The petition, 'Give us this day our daily bread' (v 11) very likely should read: 'Give us today our bread for the coming day', that is to say, the bread of the banquet in the kingdom.

The plea for the forgiveness of all sins ('debts') also looks to the end, when Sin will be no more. And, we pray not be crushed by the great Temptation, the End-time crisis, to escape, at last and forever, the designs of the Evil One. From first to last it is a prayer of faith and hope, a prayer that looks confidently beyond this world to the Rule of the Father. The plea for forgiveness in v 12 is underscored by the codicil of vv 13-14. The implication is that we are expected to forgive others before we plead for God's forgiveness of us. (See Sirach 28:1-5). Indeed (as the prayer stands) we make our forgiveness of others a condition of God's forgiveness of us. The commentary simply makes unmistakable the sense of the petition: 'For if you forgive others their trespasses, your heavenly Father will also forgive you; but if you do not forgive others, neither will your Father forgive your trespasses' (6:14-15). The obligation of forgiveness cannot be stressed more clearly. Well for us that God does not really temper his boundless mercy to our grudging forgiveness. But what he expects of us is clear.

TEACHINGS 6:19-7:12

There is no obvious structure to the third part of the Sermon (6:19-7:12). We will look at some sections of it. In 6:19-34 Jesus cautions his disciples against worldly standards: the 'treasures' of the world are tawdry and fragile. What Jesus calls for is 'purity of heart'. A person's heart is where one's treasure is (6:21) There is a basic decision: one must choose to worship ('serve') the one true God, the heavenly Father, or the false god of worldly possessions. Jesus came to reveal the Father to men and women, to assure them that they are not alone. The Father loves them and cares for them. We are in constant danger of becoming immersed in the affairs of this world and of allowing them to enslave us. Here Jesus calls on us to pass beyond a care for material things to a consideration of higher values. Humankind is made for God and only in God can we find rest.

The general theme of the passage is expressed in a wealth of imagery that is typically Matthean (Matthew tends to work with pairs of images). The wild flowers and grasses shape a particularly telling image of transience. After the rains in Palestine there is a short period when the arid and rocky scrub soil is covered with delicate wild flowers. In a few weeks they have withered to yellow, brittle stalks of hay.

Jesus' words are meant to highlight the reality of God's care. God is not an impersonal force remote from this world. He is very much present, even when he may seem to be absent. Jesus is not condemning human industry or resourcefulness. We must plan for the morrow. The beauty of the lilies fades and birds die of hunger. We, too, will shrivel unless we use our God-given talents.

What Jesus calls on us to avoid is not the normal concern demanded by our human condition but the fretting that dehumanises us, the worry that keeps us from lifting our gaze beyond material values and the cares of this world. The concluding proverb (v 34) is not really as enigmatic as it sounds. Each day has its burden of problems; it does not help to add the morrow's problems to the load. The Christian will look not to a fleeting 'tomorrow' but to the solid future of the kingdom. We will put our future in the hands of God and pray only for the modest needs of today.

A caution; we are not to be too ready to pass judgment on others. It is so easy to spot the faults of others. A touch of humour: if we could but see ourselves – many of us walking about with big planks sticking out of our eyes, while we peer at a speck in our neighbour's eye! (7:1-5). As for prayer: ask… seek… knock! – even though your Father knows your need before you ask (see 6:8). Why ask then? God does not need our prayer. We need God; we need to acknowledge our dependence; we must seek and knock. The need is ours. Think of mother and child: a loving mother knows what is best for her child. The child may ask, may demand; but she will give only what is helpful. A firm 'no' is often the most loving answer. We should never forget that 'no' is quite as much an answer as 'yes' – even to prayer!

THE CLOSE 7:13-29

The road to the kingdom is no four-lane highway – there is a narrow gate at the end of it. In 7:13-14 the motif of the two gates is joined with that of the two ways. Each way leads to a gate: to perdition or to eternal life. This motif of the Two Ways was traditional in the ancient world. In the Old Testament it is found most prominently in Deut 11:26-28; 30:15-20. There is a stark choice. It is Matthews's view that entrance to the kingdom is difficult; not many will get there. He reflects the pessimism of 4 Ezra: 'I said before, and I say now, and will say it again: There are more who perish than those who will be saved, as a wave is greater than a drop of water' (9:15-16). It is scarcely the view of Jesus. The traumatic event of 70 AD scarred both the author of 4 Ezra and Matthew. We must constantly remind ourselves that, though we have to think and speak and write of God in anthropomorphic terms, God is *divine*! We speak, casually of a God 'of infinite love'. Do we take that *infinite* seriously? Surely not – however could we have come up with the ultimate blasphemy: a God who condemns sinners to hell? To return to Matthew. It is his view that those who will not find their way through the narrow gate are false prophets. Their fruits will show them up (Mt 7:15-20).

The passage 7:21-23 speaks against a hazard of any official religion. The essential demand is to do the will of God. But people can pretend to be religious and pious while failing hopelessly to fulfil the revealed will of God as enunciated in the extended teaching of the

Sermon. The wearing of religious titles is no guarantee of true
uprightness in the eyes of God. Not every one who addresses Christ
by his faith-name, 'Lord', can be assured of partaking in God's
reign. Religion must be more than a superficial display. Use of religious language and ritual do not necessarily accomplish the new
righteousness and measure up to the moral requirements of the
kingdom.

Jesus' words of condemnation are strong and unexpected: 'I never
knew you; go away from me, you evildoers.' 'Knowledge' in the
Bible is very often the knowledge of personal relationship. It has
overtones of love and attachment: the knowledge which friends
have of one another, the mutual knowledge of husband and wife.
This kind of knowledge presupposes the mutual self-gift of one
person to the other. So Jesus can say 'I never knew you' because the
condemned did not make their contribution to the relationship.
They remained aloof by following their own mirages of religious
responsibility. The Sermon concludes with a contrast-parable (vv
24-27).

Jesus contrasts the person who responds to his teaching with the
one who does not. One who fulfils his words is like a man who built
his house on a solid rock foundation. In the moment of crisis he can
withstand all assaults and temptations because he has made the
teaching of Christ the basis of his moral life. But the person who
does not act on his teaching cannot boast of any such moral integrity
or stability. That one is like a man who has built his house on the
sandy bed of a river (the dry Palestinian *wadi* or watercourse).
When the (winter) floods come it collapses under the force of the
flood waters. If a person is to survive the crises of one's moral life,
particularly the supreme crisis before the end (the apocalyptic perspective), one must adhere to the teaching of Christ. 'These words
of mine': the authority is no longer the Torah of Moses but the
teaching of Jesus – including his reinterpretation of Torah.

CHAPTER 5

Mission in Galilee

A disciple is not above the teacher (Mt 10:24)

HEALINGS 8-9

The Sermon had shown Jesus powerful in word, a word that astounded his hearers (7:28). Now, Matthew sets out to demonstrate his power to heal. Jesus' reputation as healer is emphatically attested by all four evangelists. This healing activity covered a range of afflictions: paralysis, blindness, deafness, leprosy and other ailments. In chs 8-9 Matthew has nine healings; all but one, the cure of the centurion's servant (8:5-13), come from Mark. He has rearranged and abbreviated them. He has included the stilling of the storm (8:23-27).[13]

The first three healings (8:1-17), at Capernaum, were of a leper, a centurion's servant and of Peter's mother-in-law: healing of an outcast Jew, healing at a Gentile's request, and healing of a woman. Jesus was displaying his special concern for the marginalised. Then (8:18-34) he crossed to the eastern shore of the lake, stilling a storm on the way – doing what God does. In the country of the Gaderenes he healed two violently insane men, two 'demoniacs', manifesting his power over evil. On returning to Capernaum (9:1) he healed a paralytic (9:2-8). This story demonstrated that Jesus could heal not only physical ailments but also the spiritual sickness of sin. The episodes of the stilling of the storm, of the exorcising of demons, and of the forgiving of sins helped to answer the disciples' question in 8:27 – 'What sort of man is this?'

There are further healings in 9:18-34. A synagogue leader pleaded for the life of his twelve-year-old daughter. On his way to the man's home, a woman suffering from a chronic haemorrhage encountered Jesus; she met him with faith and was healed. Matthew, despite radical abbreviation (see Mk 5:21-43) has preserved the main drift of the episode: on faith and salvation (Mt 9:18-26). This is, notably, in the exchange between the woman and Jesus. She had said to herself: 'If I only touch his cloak, I will be made well.' Jesus said to her, 'Take heart, daughter; your faith has made you well' (vv 21-22). Each time the verb is *sózó* which means also 'to save'. Matthew has in mind more than bodily healing. But, salvation comes in close relation to faith. Two blind men cried out for mercy to the 'Son of David.' They responded to his challenge to faith and were recompensed: 'According to your faith let it be done to you' (9:27-31). The reaction to Jesus' healing of a deaf-mute was the amazed chorus of the crowd: 'Never has anything like this been seen in Israel!' (9:32-33). The Pharsisees were not impressed: 'By the ruler of the demons he casts out the demons' (9:34). Matthew sounds a note of warning. The opposition to Jesus will be developed in his next narrative section (chs 11-12).

The Physician 9:10-13

The compassion of Jesus, manifest in his healings, is highlighted by the passage 9:10-13 set among the healing stories. That scene, Jesus' meal with 'tax collectors and sinners', follows naturally from the call of Matthew, a tax-collector (9:9). The passage illustrates that Jesus' attitude towards outcasts was a scandal to the religious authorities. We know that tablefellowship (between Christians of Jewish and of Gentile backgrounds) was something of a problem in the early church (see Acts 11:3; Gal 2:12), and it would have been crucial in the matter of eucharistic tablefellowship. It may well be · that this interest accounts for the formation and preservation of the original story.

The Pharisees (the 'separated ones') regarded Jesus' openly shared meals with tax collectors and sinners – people whose lifestyle surely did not meet proper religious standards – as scandalous behaviour. In the gospels the Pharisees, for historical and polemical reasons, get a bad press. They are cast as legalistic rigorists with little respect for people, with contempt for ordinary folk.

This is less than fair. Jesus had a good deal in common with Pharisees. And, where the gospels might seem to give the impression that the Pharisees are those mainly responsible for the death of Jesus, it was, in fact, the Jerusalem priestly authorities (not Pharisees) who, together with Roman authorities, engineered the death of Jesus. The prevalent view of Pharisees has exaggerated their influence and misrepresented their religious outlook. Given, however, their perception of themselves as people of the law, they would count themselves guardians of the law and of the ancestral customs. Zeal for the law became an identity marker of the 'sect' of the Pharisees. It is reasonable, then, to take 'sinners' as a functional term, describing those whose conduct was regarded as unacceptable to a sectarian mentality.

This brings us back to the conduct of Jesus and to the charge against him. A welcome, on his part, for repentant sinners who had made amends, who had 'paid their debt to society,' would have been quite acceptable to the 'righteous' – whatever else they might have thought of Jesus. The scandal was that he associated with sinners and rejoiced in their company. He did not call them to repent as normally understood, which involved restitution (in personal offences) and a formal offering of sacrifice in the Temple. He asked only that they accept his message – which offered them the kingdom. This was the scandal – a fatal scandal for Jesus – of the righteous. Jesus preached forgiveness rather than repentance. And he turned forgiveness into celebration (Lk 15:7, 10, 22-24, 32; 23:43).

In dining with tax-collectors and 'sinners', the pariah elements of contemporary society, Jesus expressed his solidarity with them. This was behaviour which elicited the objection of the Pharisees. The Matthean Jesus' reply, recalling Hos 6:6, shows that the correct attitude to social dropouts is not one of sequestration and condemnation but of familiarity and service. The Pharisees are seen as the hypocrites of Hosea's day who were assiduous at attending the liturgy of the sanctuaries while they ground the faces of the poor. They did not realise that the word 'liturgy' means, precisely, 'service', in both senses of service of God in the liturgy and the service of humans by love. Jesus revealed that these are two sides of the same coin.

The Pharisees' rightful insistence on purity should, if it be a matter of true holiness, have pressed them to help the 'unenlightened'. Jesus' association with the 'outlaws' of his day was not tantamount to a condonation of their actions or situation; rather, he associated with them in order to raise their sights, to show them a new life. But he could not do this unless he were sympathetic towards them.

Against the background of the Old Testament, where Yahweh alone is Physician (see Hos 14:4; Jer 3:22; 17:4; 30:17; Sir 38:1-15) and healing a sign of the messianic age (see Is 61:1; Mt 10:1, 8), Jesus' reference to himself as 'physician' (Mt 9:12) implies more than a proverbial justification of his conduct: if he eats with sinners it is because the sick have need of the Physician. For those who can see, his action is a declaration that the messianic age has dawned: the Physician has come.

The saying of v 13b ('for I have come not to call the righteous, but sinners') infers that messianic forgiveness is the basis of tablefellowship. And the truth was, as the early Christians were well aware, that the saving call of Jesus had been to sinners. It was for this that Jesus had come into the world, to summon such as they to the messianic banquet. This was the comforting assurance addressed to all who have ever heard the call of Jesus (see Jn 1:8-10). The first Christians knew that the church was made up of sinners. This is a fact of life of the earthly church.

MISSION SERMON 10:5-42

Introduction 9:36-10:4

Sight of a leaderless crowd moves Jesus to think of the need for a mission by his disciples. The kingdom of God has come, the last age, and the mission of bringing the good news to others, of gathering believers into his community, is part of the great final event. It is a task that will challenge Christians while this world lasts. Indeed, we see the harvest-field grow wider and more lush decade by decade. It could be a discouraging task, given the immensity of the harvest (all humankind) and the handful of missionaries. The workers should not yield to discouragement. The Father, the Lord of the harvest, is in control. They should ask him to send out labourers. Prayer becomes a missionary work. The church was true to this word of the Lord when it proclaimed a Carmelite contemplative nun (Thérèse of Lisieux) patroness of the missions.

That helpless multitude (9:36) is the backdrop to the choice of twelve disciples who would continue Jesus' own messianic work. They will alert people to the advent of the kingdom and the availability of salvation. Like Jesus, they too are endowed with the ability to relieve human need, 'to cure every disease and every sickness' as a sign and pledge of a more fundamental salvation. They also share Jesus' messianic authority to loosen evil's stranglehold on humankind. For the moment, they are given an apprentice mission. Like Jesus himself (15:24), they are to go only 'to the lost sheep of the house of Israel.' After the death-resurrection, however, they will be formally commissioned by the risen Lord to undertake a universal mission.

Mission to Israel 10:5-15

'I was sent only to the lost sheep of the house of Israel' (15:24). Jesus firmly stated the firm limits of the range of his mission. He adhered to the salvation-historical precedence of Israel. His instructions to the Twelve, not surprisingly then, include the same limitation: their mission is to 'the lost sheep of the house of Israel.'

The mission of the disciples mirrors that of Jesus. The proclamation of the kingdom is the same: 'The kingdom of heaven has come near' (see 4:17). They are to cure the sick, raise the dead, cleanse lepers and cast out demons – just as Jesus had done. Significantly, there is no mandate to teach. They can teach confidently only whey they have received the full teaching of Jesus – 'teaching them to obey *everything* that I have commanded you' (28:20). Because the disciples had received their call and commission and the gifts that went them 'without payment' (v 8) they must demand no payment. Instead, in their fidelity to mission, they will earn and deserve support (see 1 Cor 9:3-12). 'Shake off the dust from your feet' (Mt 9:14): Jews would shake off Gentile dust when they returned, from abroad, to the Holy Land. Here the point is that those who will not hearken to the gospel (good news) are no better than pagans. The strong language of v 15 carries a distinctive Matthean theme: judg-

ment is severe for those who have heard the good news but have
failed to act upon it.

The emphasis on a mission to Israel is of particular concern to
Matthew's community. It viewed itself as the authentic way of
Judaism after 70 AD. It wanted fellow Jews to see the light.
Matthew works on two levels. One is confined to the time and char-
acters of his narrative world (the ministry of Jesus). The other
reaches beyond to the reader who reads the text with the eyes of
resurrection-faith. This is why, despite the seeming limitation here,
a mission to the Gentiles is emphatically in place (28:19). A contemporary mission to Israel is not at all excluded.

> Christianity's continuing mission to Israel remains a very deli-
> cate matter in Christian-Jewish relations. On the one hand, the
> mission to the Gentiles (Mt 28:19) does not exclude the mission
> to Israel (10:5b-6). Indeed, if Christians are convinced of the
> rightness and importance of the gospel, they are obliged to
> share it with others, including and especially Jews. On the other
> hand, the history of the Christian mission to Israel with its per-
> secutions, forced conversions, and insensitive approaches to
> evangelisation have correctly made most Jews suspicious of
> such a mission. In its third millennium Christianity needs to
> find a better way both to be faithful to the gospel mandate and
> to be sensitive in its efforts in carrying out that mandate.[14]

Trials 10:16-25

'A disciple is not above the teacher, nor a slave above the master'
(10:24). The missionaries have been told that they will share the
mission and authority of Jesus; now they are told that they will par-
ticipate in his rejection and persecution and, it may be, in his death.
This is spelled out in 10:17-22, a text which very closely follows Mk
13:9-13. Noteworthy is the threefold repetition of *paradidómi*, 'to
deliver up' (vv 17, 19, 21): persecution and suffering are their lot,
serving a divine purpose. They will be haled before Jewish tri-
bunals (v 17) and Gentile authorities (v 18). Paradoxically, as pris-
oners on trial, they bear witness to the Name. They are promised
help (vv 19-20). It is not said that the Spirit will speak up on their
behalf. Rather, the help of the Spirit means that the preparation of

the defence is less an apologia than a prayer. Most painful of all is the factor of family division (vv 21-22). This had become a commonplace of apocalyptic (e.g. 2 Bar 70:3; 4 Ezra 5; 9). Here, however, denunciation from within would suggest the experience of Jewish Christians after 70 AD: they found themselves at loggerheads with other family members. The saying of v 23 envisages an imminent coming of the Son of Man – a prevalent expectation in the early church (see Mk 9:1; 13:30). It is not clear how Matthew would have understood it. V 25 states the principle underlying the passage: as disciples and slaves Christians cannot expect a better fate than that of their teacher and master.

Trust in God 10:26-33

The missionaries have a role very like that of Jeremiah and the other prophets, whose successors they are (5:12). For, the Good News which they are to preach is not 'good' for everyone. In this passage, towards the end of the mission sermon, Jesus exhorts his disciples to fearless and confident proclamation of the gospel in the teeth of persecution. 'Do not fear' is a refrain (vv 26, 28, 31): the preachers are to fear God only, not human beings; they are to trust in God's care of them. The disciple of Christ must steadfastly proclaim the teaching of the Master and faithfully bear witness to him. The apostle must not fall silent; one may not avoid fearless confession of one's faith. On the contrary, one must seek every opportunity of communicating the saving message of Jesus. One must preach from the housetops and gain the maximum attention for one's words.

These gospel words do not promise the witness of Christ that he or she will escape suffering or even martyrdom. Indeed, all who wish to remain true to the gospel must be prepared to suffer (see 2 Tim 3:12). But the Lord who knows every detail of the lives of his witnesses will take special care of them in every trial and support them in every crisis. If, in their turn, they are faithful, they will meet Jesus' approval at the final tribunal. A warning sounds for one who will have shrunk from bearing witness to Christ: such a one will not be acknowledged as a true child of the Father.

Commitment 10:34-39

Jesus had come to offer peace. Paradoxically, the challenge of his good news brings strife. This is due to rejection of the good news. Family dissension emerges again: a dramatic presentation of the divisions he occasions. It echoes Micah 7:6. The theme of suffering re-emerges (v 38). Jesus did not shrink from the cross; the faithful disciple will be ready to shoulder it. 'Life' (*psyché*) means both 'life' and 'self'. The meaning of the paradoxical saying (v 39) is that one who, through fear of losing one's (earthly) life, denies Jesus and thus thinks to save oneself, in reality loses one's eschatological life ('eternal life', Jn 12:25) in God. It is the paradox of the cross.

Recompense 10:40-42

It is a rabbinical principle that 'the representative of a person is as the person.' Jesus, as the 'one sent', is the Father's representative; the disciples, sent by him, are his representatives. V 42 gives the assurance that the smallest act of kindness shown to a disciple on the ground of one's being a disciple of Christ will not fail to have its reward. What is presupposed is a gracious God who will not over-look the slightest deed of generosity. 'Reward' is not something we earn: it is always free gift of a generous God. In vv 40-42 it is arguable that Matthew has established an order which may reflect the structure of his community. We get: apostles ('you'), prophets, the righteous person (a prominent member), little ones (the 'simple faithful'). Matthew closes the discourse with his customary transi-tional formula (11:1).

CHAPTER 6

The Hidden Kingdom 11-13

Let anyone with ears listen! (Mt 13: 9)

OPPOSITION AND DIVISION CHS 11-12

Who is John the Baptist? 11:2-29 The mission of the Baptist (3:1-17) had inaugurated the ministry of Jesus. As Jesus resumes his mission after his instruction of the Twelve the Baptist is reintroduced. Matthew compares John and Jesus and stresses the rejection of both by their people. The relationship between Jesus and John is illustrated in question and answer (11:2-6), in Jesus' assessment of John (vv 7-1) and in the rejection of both John and Jesus (vv 16-19).

John the Baptist, in prison (see 4:12), has a problem (11:2-3). His question was prompted by the fact that, in his eyes, the coming Messiah was an awesome judge of he end-time (3:12); Jesus' approach was so different from anything he had expected. John himself was a prophet of doom who warned that the axe was laid to the root of the trees; hence, 'every tree that does not bear good fruit is cut down and thrown into the fire' (3:10). Furthermore, he is convinced that the Coming One would follow his line: 'His winnowing fork is in his hand... the chaff he will burn with unquenchable fire' (3:12). In point of fact, Jesus proclaimed that 'the kingdom of God is at hand' (Mk 1:15). Where John prophesied the judgment of God, Jesus prophesied the salvation of God. Hearing, in prison, of the activity of Jesus, a perplexed John sent two of his disciples to enquire: 'Are you the one who is to come, or are we to wait for another?' (Mt 11:2). And the answer was: 'Go and tell John what you hear and see: the blind receive their sight, the lame walk, the lepers are cleansed, the deaf hear, the dead are raised, and the poor have good news brought to them' (11:4-5). In effect, the answer is that, while Jesus does not fit the unsparing role the Baptist envisaged, he is attuned to another prophetical tradition. Jesus reminds John (through John's disciples) that he had not come to condemn but to save and that healing forgiveness and redemption are the hallmark of God's judgment. John is a prophet of doom, in the line of Amos, Jesus is a prophet of love and forgiveness, spokesman of the Spouse and Father (Mother) in the manner of Hosea (see Hos 1-3; 11).

How is one to evaluate the Baptist? One is not likely to improve on Jesus' assessment (11:7-19). Jesus' testimony firmly relates John to God's plan of salvation. The rhetorical questions ('What did you go out into the wilderness to look at?', 11:7, 8, 9) serve to define – in terms of what John was not – the role of the Baptist. John is no reed bending to every breeze but a granite figure; he is no flaccid courtier but a prisoner of conscience in Herod's dungeon. He is indeed a prophet, a spokesman of God. For that matter, he is 'more than a prophet' because as *Elijah redivivus* (v 14) he is precursor of Jesus and because no other, not even one of the prophets of old, is greater than he. The further statement – 'yet the least in the kingdom of God is greater then he' (v 28) – does not cancel the unique status of John. Rather, the contrast is between the age of promise and the age of fulfilment.

We can picture the little scene that Jesus describes in 11:16. The children, *sitting* in the marketplace – the boys playing the flute and the girls chanting a funeral dirge – form part of a game. The remaining boys are expected to dance (the round dance at weddings was performed by men) and the rest of the girls ought to have formed a funeral procession. Since they have failed to do so, the others loudly complain that they are spoilsports. The point of the parable, then, is the frivolous captiousness of these children and the thrust of it is obvious: the conduct of the scribes and Pharisees is no better. At the moment of crisis, when the last messengers of God had appeared, they hearkened neither to the preaching of repentance nor to the proclamation of the Good News, but criticised and sulked. This was the experience of Matthew and his community in respect of their fellow Jewish adversaries.

Revelation of Father and Son 11:25-30

Mention of Jesus at prayer is relatively frequent in the gospels but only rarely, in the synoptics, are we given any words of his prayer. Matthew and Luke have preserved this lovely prayer of his (Mt 11:25-26; Lk 10:21). It is prayer which brings consolation to all the 'little ones' who feel that they have done nothing more than believe. If they have indeed listened they have already done a 'good work.' Their achievement may seem, in their eyes, a small thing. Because it is gift of the Father, it is of priceless worth. Both evangelists go on, in strangely Johannine terms, to stress the unique relationship of Father and Son, and to explain why Jesus had joyfully thanked the Father for his gracious gift to the little ones (Mt 11:27; Lk 10:22). Equality of Father and Son underlines the unique sonship of Jesus. That Son now invites his disciples to a share in his sonship – there is a comforting glow to his gracious invitation (Mt 11:28-30). There is an echo of Old Testament personified Wisdom (see Prov 8-9; Sir 51:23-27). A two-fold invitation is matched by a two-fold promise. Or, rather, the invitation is 'come... and take' and the promise is 'rest'. Jewish rabbis spoke of the 'yoke of the Torah' – a yoke which, because of the unwieldy 'tradition of men' raised on the law of Moses (see Mk 7:6-8), had become an intolerable burden (Acts 15:10). The 'yoke' of Jesus is the demand for love of God and neighbour (Mt 22:34-40) – and 'his commandments are not burdensome' (1 Jn 5:3). His yoke is easy and his burden is light because of who he is – one 'gentle and humble in heart.' He is no taskmaster but a Master who is a Friend (Jn 15:14-15). He finds his 'meat', his fulfilment, in doing the will of the Father (Jn 4:34). In that will is the disciple of the Son to find rest.

> The spiritual rest Jesus gives (cf Jer 6:16) comes not from practicing 613 commandments, but from assimilating and living Jesus' attitudes, indeed, his very person. In Jesus the Wisdom of God, the teacher and the subject taught are one and the same. Adherence to his person is the sum-total of the law, a yoke that proves most light to the true disciple.[15]

Chapter 12

Most of Matthew 12 is drawn from the conflict stories of Mark 2:1-3:6. In Matthew, however, there is bitter controversy as Jesus hits back. In Mt 12:1-8 the clash between Jesus and the Pharisees is over one's image of God. Is God a legalist who goes by the book, or a God of liberating mercy? The Hosea-like prophet Jesus quotes Hosea: 'I desire mercy and not sacrifice.' In Mt 12:9 Jesus entered *their* synagogue: Matthew's community had broken with Judaism. The message of vv 10-13 is that mercy is lawful on the sabbath – a touch of irony. Aware of a plot to get rid of him, Jesus withdrew – yet carried on his healing mission. This occasions Matthew's longest fulfilment citation (12:18-21; see Is 42:1-4). The meek and merciful servant, Jesus, is responding to the divine will.

The intransigence of the Pharisees surfaces in 12:24 when they purport to see the hand of Beelzebub in Jesus' exorcisms. In vv 33-37 Jesus sternly denounces them. They are bad trees bearing the evil fruit of malicious words. They will be held to account. In vv 38-42 Jesus rejects the request for a sign. The resurrection of Jesus, typified by Jonah, will be the only sign God will grant. The pagan Ninevites repented at the summons of an insignificant Jewish prophet (Jonah 3:4-10); the Pharisees will not listen to a far greater prophet. The queen of the South undertook a long journey to hear the wisdom of Solomon; the Pharisees have turned a deaf ear to the greater than Solomon among them.

Jesus had freed people of 'unclean spirits'. The 'house' of the healed person is now 'swept, and put in order.' It should not remain empty but become a dwelling of God in the Spirit (see Eph 2:22). Otherwise there is the danger of a disastrous re-possession. Jesus has broken Satan's hold over Israel. If Israel does not acknowledge its messianic deliverer, its state will be worse than ever. For Matthew, the destruction of Jerusalem was a measure of that disaster.

SERMON IN PARABLES CH 13

Chapter 13 is pivotal in Matthews's gospel. What we find is that just as Jesus used parables to meet the demands of his own situation, so does Matthew use them to meet the needs of his community. He has put the parables of ch 13 at the service of his own age and of his own theology. The parable passage forms the second part of the whole section 11:2-13:53. Part one (chs 11-12) records the mounting opposition to Jesus and the rejection of him by the leaders of the people. This is underlined by the words of thanksgiving for the revelation to 'infants' of what remains hidden to 'the wise and the intelligent' (11:25-26), and culminates in the passage about the 'true relatives' of Jesus, those who do the will of the Father (12:46-50). Then, in 13:1-15, Jesus addresses the 'crowds' as representing the whole of unbelieving Judaism – those who are blind, deaf, lacking understanding (13:10-13). Matthew is saying that the first half of Jesus' parable discourse is an apologia; it is his reaction to his having been rejected by the Jews. But the second half of the discourse (13:36-52) marks a sudden shift to the *disciples* (13:36). They are such as do God's will (13:49-50). Jesus instructs them as to what doing God's will really means.

Parables

At least in his chapter 13, Matthew's use of *parable* seems to conform to that of Mark in two respects. Matthew regards the parable as an enigmatic form of speech directed primarily at outsiders. He distinguishes between a time when Jesus addressed the Jews openly and a time when he begins to address them in parables. In particular, he suggests that Jesus' reply to his rejection by the Jews was distinctively parabolic in form. Jesus had come to the Jews, preaching and teaching, but was rejected by them. He reacted by addressing his apologia to them, but in parables, that is, in riddle, in speech for outsiders. By this fact he proclaims that the Jews are no longer the privileged people of God but, rather, stand under judgment for having spurned their Messiah. This factor (Jesus' turning from the Jews and towards his disciples) is the great turning-point of the gospel; Matthew uses his parable chapter to mark the turning-point. But, for him, this is not a matter of past history: it has immediate relevance for the church to which he belongs. It reflects the relationship, one of virulent animosity, between his Jewish Christian community and contemporary Pharisaic Judaism. While the evangelist does consider the leaders of Judaism to be incorrigible, radically closed to the saving message of Jesus, the same does not hold true for the Jewish people as such. The people of the Jews may still be evangelised and the gospel is addressed to them.

In chapter 13, Matthew called attention to the great turning-point in several ways. For one thing, he studiously avoids designating

Jesus' speech in parables to the Jews as teaching (*didaskein*) or preaching (*keryssein*); instead, he describes it as *lalein*, that is, a 'speaking.' Furthermore, Matthew consistently refers to the Jewish crowds in 13:1-35 as 'them' (*autois*); he thereby depicts the (unbelieving) Jews as a people that stands outside the circle of those to whom God imparts his revelation and promises his end-time kingdom. He introduced the term *parabolé* for the first time in chapter 13 and then distinguishes between a time when Jesus spoke openly to the Jews and a time when he began to speak to them enigmatically. Finally, he gathered eight parabolic units (and two explanations), provided a framework for them, and so drafted a parable speech in two parts.[16]

The Sower 13:3-9, 18-23

The parable of the sower (13:3-9) might, just as well, be called the parable of the soils because, throughout, the emphasis is not really on sower or seed but on the different kinds of soil on which the seed falls. As a parable this is not, as might seem, an agricultural vignette. And the situation depicted is not typically Palestinian as has frequently been urged. Instead one should take the peculiar actions of the sower as part of the deliberately unusual dimension of the story.

The early church's explanation of the parable (vv 18-23) takes it to be concerned with 'the word of the kingdom'. This word is sown in the hearers. Four categories of hearers are distinguished in terms of the place where the seed has fallen: 'on the path', 'on rocky ground', 'among thorns', and 'on good soil'. The fate of the word differs in each case. The evil one comes and snatches the word as it is preached (v 19). Initial joy at the hearing of the word will not compensate for lack of root. Here is a person of the moment who will not persevere in the face of tribulation and persecution (vv 20-21). The description of the third person (v 22) is the analysis of a moralist who leans in great part on explicit teaching of Jesus. The fourth person (v 23) suggests that it is enough to be good soil, to be receptive, in order to bring forth fruit. The application is not unfaithful to the parable, for it only takes the subjective aspect of the proclamation and applies it to the hearers. They are shown that the story of the sower does concern them.

The explanation came about because Christians had discovered to their shock and sorrow that few really believed Jesus' message. They asked the burning question: how could it be that there was such a gulf between themselves and those who could not or would not see? They found an answer in the words of the parable. Think what happens when the sower scatters his seed. Much is lost, for one reason or another. Similarly, many are like the person on the pathway: the word cannot reach them, it is swiped away. Or many prove to be shallow – ready enough to receive, but the readiness did not persist. Many are like seed under thorns: they hear, but the word fights a losing battle against cares and distractions. The shallow mind, the wayward heart, worldly preoccupations, persecution – all these are the obstacles which frustrate the growth of faith. The explanation offers a warning and an encouragement (the harvest) to Christians in such conditions.

Seed Parables 13:24-35

The parable of the weeds among the wheat (13:24-30, 36- 43) – whatever its original intent in the preaching of Jesus – is intended by Matthew as a description of the church, as a reminder that it is not a community of the elect and eternally secure, but a mixed body of righteous and unrighteous, all of whom stand under the mercy of God. It is a parable of the 'kingdom of heaven'. The kingdom is not primarily a state or place but rather the dynamic event of God coming in power to rule his people Israel in the end-time. It should however, and can, become a reality here and now. God's rule becomes real when it finds expression in human life.[17] In its present form is not yet ready for the harvest. Nor has the harvest time arrived. For the present there are good and bad within the kingdom itself. It is only at the judgment that the separation between the two kinds will take place (13:30, 49-50). Emphasis is on the coexistence of good and bad within the kingdom. Because the parable is intended as a repudiation of any elitist or purist view of the kingdom it contains a message of hope. As long as the kingdom is growing, it remains possible to change from 'weed' into 'wheat'. For that matter, part of the message of the parable is to exhort the 'weeds' to change.

Between the parable of the weeds and its explanation, Matthew presents two parables with the same message: the contrast between the small, unpromising beginnings of the kingdom (the preaching of Jesus) and a glorious result (the Kingdom of God). These parables (vv 31-32, 33) would have been the answer of Jesus to an objection, latent or expressed: could the kingdom really come from such inauspicious beginnings? His reply is that the little cell of disciples will indeed become a kingdom. And in the last analysis, if the kingdom does reach its full dimension, it is not due to anything in the men and women who are the seed of the kingdom; the growth is due solely to the power of God (see 1 Cor 3:6-7) This is why Jesus can speak with utter confidence of the final stage of the kingdom. And that is why these parables are a call to patience.

Besides, Matthew has an apologetic intent. Contrary to Jewish belief, Jesus declares that the kingdom *has* come in his person, though, because of its humble beginnings, not as they had expected it. He sounds a paraenetic note: the Lord fortifies the Christians of Matthew's church in the conviction that they *are* the eschatological community. The words on Jesus' use of parables (vv 34-35) conclude the first half of Matthew's parable discourse. It anchors Jesus' use of parables in salvation history: the sermon in parables is fulfilment of prophecy. Jesus thereby testifies to his messiahship and the claim of his church in his regard is vindicated.

For the Disciples 13:36-52

'Then he left the crowds and went into the house' (13:36). It is a major change of setting. The second half of the parable discourse is directed solely to the disciples. Therefore, Matthew chooses for Jesus the privacy of a house. The explanation of the parable of the weeds (vv 36-43) is manifestly later than the parable and, very likely, is Matthew's creation. The Lord exhorts the Christians of Matthew's community to be children of the kingdom who do God's will. Here Matthew's ethical concern is bolstered by apocalyptic imagery. This shows how the evangelist regards eschatology as bound up with ethics. That is to say, the coming Age exerts a pressure which works itself out in the practical life of Christians. So, the old-style mission hell-fire sermon was meant to have a salutary effect on the daily lives of the hearers. That the effect was salutary is questionable.

The parables of the treasure and the pearl (vv 44, 45-46), closely related and proper to Matthew, are linked by the formula 'the kingdom of heaven is like.' The key to them is found in the phrase 'in his joy' (v 44). A poor farm-labourer had profited from the fate of some wealthy man who, in a moment of crisis, had hidden his valuables but (most likely) had lost his life. The finder does not hesitate. He has to sell everything he has – but he *must* have that treasure. The pearl merchant has found what he had dreamt of: the *perfect* pearl. Gladly he sells his caravan or his ship (depending on whether he was a merchant on land or sea) to get that pearl. To an outsider, the conduct of peasant and merchant must seem crazy. But *they* know that their course of action is the only one that makes sense. They had discovered the treasure of the kingdom and had realised that it is worth any price. What seems crazy to others is, to them, the only sensible way to act. Note: there is no stress here on sacrifice. Both men gladly give their all because they *know* that they have found so much more.

The parable of the dragnet (vv 47-50) conveys basically the same message as that of the wheat and the weeds (13:24-30, 36-41): the kingdom at the present time contains both 'good' and 'bad'; it is only at the end that a separation will be made. By placing his emphasis on judgment, Matthew sounds a note of warning.

THE CONCLUSION

At the end of the discourse (vv 51-53) the readers are drawn into a parable, one that has to do with understanding. Matthew considers understanding to be essential to the making of a disciple. In Mark the disciples are devoid of understanding until the resurrection of Jesus; in Matthew they, true children of the kingdom, understand and accept the message of the kingdom. One who has become a disciple of the kingdom knows and understands both the old (the Old Testament) and the new (the Good News) and is in a position to see God's promises in the Old Testament fulfilled in Christ (which is what Matthew does in his gospel). Matthew, at the close, presents his description of a Christian of his community who treasures the old (the Jewish heritage) and the new (the good news of and from Jesus). It may, consciously or not, be a self-portrait.

CHAPTER 7

The Kingdom Develops 14-18

Unless you change and become like children (Mt 18:3)

FORMATION OF DISCIPLES 13:53-17:27

After the Sermon in parables (ch 13) Jesus' ministry in Galilee resumes (13:54-58). From this point on, Matthew follows closely the sequence of Mark. Coming to his hometown, Nazareth, Jesus entered 'their' synagogue. At first his teaching caught his towns-folk's surprised attention. Quickly they concluded that he was nothing more than one of themselves. Matthew then (14:1-12) gives a much abbreviated version of Mark's dramatic narrative of the death of the Baptist (Mk 6:14-29).

Feeding of Five Thousand 14:13-21

This miracle of 'the loves and fishes' should be seen as a sign. Our preoccupation with miracle as a happening beyond the laws of nature and (for a gospel miracle) as an event which 'proves' that Jesus was God's envoy – or, worse, that he is Son of God – would seem incredibly naive to the New Testament writers. The miracle stories of the gospels are addressed to people who know that Jesus was God's envoy, who *worship* the risen Lord. The miracle stories are meant to strengthen and elucidate the faith of the readers and hearers.

The sign of 'the loaves and fishes' reveals that Jesus is a new, mes-sianic Moses who nourishes God's people in the desert. The setting is explicit: the 'lonely place' of v 13 is a *desert* place, and recalls the manna (Ex 16:12-35). 'You give them something to eat': the disciples had some provisions; the loaves were likely of barley (see Jn 6:9) and the fish cured. There is a striking parallel in 2 Kgs 4:42-44. Elisha, confident that the Lord will take care, proposes to feed a hundred men with twenty barley loaves. One might see Jesus, too, as the good shepherd of Ezekiel 34 who feeds his sheep.

It was customary for a Jewish host, at the start of a meal, to pronounce a blessing over the bread and then to break it and distribute it to his guests. If the number was large, others would help in the distribution. Here the disciples do play an active role: Jesus has shown then how to care for people's needs. 'Taking–blessed–broke–gave' is consciously eucharistic language. The correspondence with 26:26 is unmistakable: 'While they were eating Jesus *took* a loaf of bread and after *blessing* it he *broke* it, *gave* it to the disciples...' This eucharistic concern explains, too, why the 'two fish' (vv 17,19) vanish abruptly. 'He looked up to heaven' (see Mk 6:41) – the origin of the words in the Roman Canon, 'and looking up to heaven' – an indication that the eucharistic reference was recognised. Like Mark, Matthew has a second feeding story (15:32-38).

Walking on the Sea 14:22-33

The first part of this episode (vv 22-27) is very like Mk 6:45-50. The incident of the walking on the waters is closely connected with the feeding of the five thousand in the synoptics and in John. It is nighttime and the boat is beaten by waves. In the Old Testament, Yahweh is the one 'who trampled the waves of the sea' (Job 9:8; see 38:16; Ps 77:19; Sir 24:5). As Matthew relates it, the story is certainly symbolic. The boat represents the church; the disciples are threatened by evil (dark) and death (the waters). Jesus is not with them, physically – but he is praying to the Father (v 23). In their need he comes to them, like Yahweh striding over the waters. But they are of little faith and fearful and they panic (v 26). Comfortingly, he assures them: 'It is I' – the Greek phrase *egó eimi*, in this epiphany context, may have some suggestion of the Johannine 'I am' sayings. In Ex 3:14 'I am' is a title of Yahweh, signifying his saving presence with his people. Jesus, then, does what God does, and speaks as God speaks.

Matthew alone adds the further episode (vv 28-33). Peter, addressing Jesus as 'Lord', seeks to share Jesus' power. He steps out confidently at first but, shaken by storm and stress, he loses heart and sinks. Yet he does still cry to the Lord – and Jesus reaches out his saving hand. Peter has merited the rebuke of Jesus ('you of little faith'): he had hesitated and panicked. He is, typically, a disciple in this present life, caught between faith and doubt (28:17). The rebuke reaches to all of us who start out courageously, only to lose heart. When Jesus (and Peter) got into the boat 'the wind ceased': his presence brought calm and peace. Those in the boat (the church) bowed down in adoration of their Lord.

Underlying the Peter-story is, very probably, the disciples' experience of the risen Lord who had come to restore their broken faith after the Passion and to bring them comfort. For Matthew, the whole passage manifests the power of faith which flows from the saving presence of Jesus. To eyes of faith, Jesus is not a ghost from the past but Son of God of the here and now. He is presence of God among men and women, sending them out into the world to bring peace and to foster true human community.

Blind Guides 15:1-20

Matthew has taken over most of Mk 7:1-23. He lays greater emphasis on 'the tradition of the elders' and, by his addition of vv 12-14, indicts the Jewish leaders. Jesus accused the Pharisee and scribes of putting their own traditions above the law of God. They had, for instance, invented a clever way of circumventing the plain command: Honour your father and your mother. They are 'hypocrites'. In v 11, the statement 'It is not what goes into the mouth that defiles a person, but it is what comes out of the mouth that defiles' is, in its manner, as sweeping as Mk 7:17-19 even though Matthew omits the 'Thus he declared all foods clean' of Mark. Jesus had not only rejected 'the tradition of the elders', he had annulled the concept of ritual purity – a blow at the heart of Judaism. This is why the disciples call Jesus' attention to the Pharisees' scandal at this radical stance. 'Let them alone': Jesus is dismissive – they are blind guides who lead others astray. Matthew's community had broken with the synagogue; the 'blind guides' had nothing to say to them.

The Canaanite Woman 15:21-28

Great faith and wry humour combine to make the Canaanite woman a memorable character. She is not daunted by the Master's restricted mission to the house of Israel and stays unperturbed by his harsh metaphor of not casting children's food to dogs. Instead, she adroitly changes the image and presses home her request. The Lord's response to her quip is warm and immediate. He praises her faith while granting her prayer.

The context of this incident is significant. In 15:1-20, in the dispute over clean and unclean, Jesus had set aside the elaborate ritual which was a wall of separation between Jew and Gentile. Now the faith of a Gentile woman in the Jewish Messiah stands in contrast to the inhibiting inflexibility of Jewish legalism. The question of the Pharisees, 'Why do your disciples break the tradition of the elders' (15:2) has a wider import than the immediate issue of ritual washings. Is Jesus departing from Israel's tradition by allowing certain attitudes in his followers (obviously a question of Matthew's own day)? The story of the Canaanite woman, in many respects, answers this question. Jesus did not step on pagan soil; the woman came from it. She comes to Israel for healing. Jesus first refuses her request on the ground that he has been sent to Israel and not to the Gentiles (v 24). There seems to be no way of softening his further saying (v 26) in reply to her repeated request; the label 'dog' was in common use among Jews as a term of contempt applied to Gentiles. Yet the story ends on a different note. The woman does not question the truth of his statement but simply points out that when the 'children' have been fed then, indeed, the 'dogs' can hope to receive their share too. She acknowledges the divinely ordained separation. If Jesus had yielded to this cry of faith even while the division between Jew and Gentile still stood, how much more, Matthew seems to be saying, must the Christian Church do so now that Jesus had broke down the barrier between the two peoples (Eph 2:14)

By coming to Jesus the woman is seeking a share in the blessings promised to the nations who recognise God's works for his people of which nothing is greater than the presence of his Son. And the evangelist knows that, on the other side of death and resurrection, the exalted Son of Man will send his disciples on a universal mission (28:16-20).

Who do you say that I am? 16:13-20

At Caesarea Philippi, the northern-most limit of historical Israel, Jesus put a leading question to his disciples: 'Who do the run of humankind take me to be' For a belief in the return of Elijah see Malachi 3:1; 4:5. As Elijah was thought to have reappeared in John the Baptist, some felt that John had returned to life in his successor, Jesus. Jeremiah and 'one of the prophets' simply means that Jesus was regarded as a prophetic figure. Jesus brushes these views aside and puts the blunt question to the disciples – and to every believer – 'But who do you say that I am.' Peter's answer is, in reality, a Christian confessional formula: 'You are the Messiah, the Son of the living God.' It goes beyond Mk 8:29 in stressing that Jesus is Son of God in a transcendent sense. The response of Jesus asserts that a mortal could never, unaided, understand or communicate the divine mystery of sonship. Peter has received a revelation.

In a passage proper to Matthew (vv 18-19) Jesus, who had received titles from Peter, now, in his turn, confers a title on Peter: he is 'the Rock'. And on the solid foundation of this rock Jesus' church will be built. The community of salvation will be preserved from the destructive power of death ('the gates of Hades'): it will last beyond this world. The image of keys (taken from Is 22:15-25) invests Peter with the power of vicegerent. He will have authority to decide, according to the teaching of Jesus, what is permissible and what is not, and the authority – always of course on truly Christian principles – to admit members to the community or, if needs be, to exclude.

Since the Sermon in parables (ch 13) Matthew has been concerned with the delineation of the kingdom of heaven. It is a mysterious, divine reality, its beginnings are humble indeed compared with its future glory. Nonetheless, the kingdom has concrete expression in the world. People are nourished within it; they embrace it in the hope of healing and divine protection The question arises, What is the kingdom? Here that question is rephrased, 'Who do people say the Son of Man is?' The evangelist tells us that it is not 'What is the kingdom? but '*Who* is the kingdom?' that is important. When we ask the question about Jesus aright then we can get the kingdom right. Jesus embodies the kingdom; everything about it refers to himself. All power in the kingdom is invested in Christ. All its authentic movements, energy, position flow from him. Once the faith of Peter has opened the apostle's heart to Jesus and so brought one into the kingdom, the kingdom's power can flow into one and, from Jesus' own lips, it flows into one in a special manner. Equally clearly, Jesus' promise to Peter is not about privilege to possess as much as duty to perform. Jesus had transformed *exousia*, authority, into *diakonia*, service. If *service* is not recognisably the pattern of authority in the church, at every level, then authority loses credibility.

If the text Mt 16:18-19 be highlighted in isolation from counterbalancing features of New Testament ecclesiology – on brother/sisterhood, mutual service, humility, diversity of charisms and so on – it results in distortion which diminishes personal dignity within the church. Besides, the New Testament is not at one as to the foundation of the church. According to 1 Cor 3:11 'No one can lay any foundation other than the one that has been laid; that foundation is Jesus Christ.' According to Eph 2:20 the household of God is 'built upon the foundation of the apostles and prophets, with Christ Jesus himself as the cornerstone.' And there is the declaration of the seer of Revelation: 'The wall of the city [the new Jerusalem] has twelve foundations, and on them the twelve names of the twelve apostles of the Lamb' (Rev 21:14) – the 'city' is a people living in the presence of God.

Suffering Discipleship 16:21-27

The opening words suggest that Jesus' prophecies of his suffering to come were ongoing. He did begin to make it clear immediately after he had elicited the first explicit expression of the disciples' faith (voiced by Peter). The evangelist's suggestion of a time-lag helps to temper the sharpness of the rebuke to Peter as well as to enhance the teaching on the true meaning of discipleship, the following of a crucified Lord

Now that Jesus and the faith of his disciples have centred the reality of the kingdom on his own person, the fate of his person is crucial for the existence of the kingdom, and will in turn deeply touch the fate of his followers. Like the other evangelists, Matthew is concerned in this passage with discipleship rather than with the foresight of Jesus. The argument is less insistent on the final fate, since Jesus is 'to be raised up on the third day,' than on the fact that this is but the *path* to the resurrection. Peter's refusal to accept this path at once withdraws him from his God-given faith; he stands across the way to the cross and thus embodies the adversary of God. The only way that Peter's faith may gain its power is for the apostle to fall in behind and tread the same path.

'And Peter took him aside' (v 22). We can picture him, in his earnestness, taking hold of Jesus and 'rebuking' him. The idea of a suffering Messiah was altogether foreign to Peter. He realises too that his own position will be affected: disciple of a suffering Messiah is not a role that would appeal to him. 'Get behind me, Satan' – the temptation in the wilderness (4:1- 11) aimed at getting Jesus himself to conform to the popularly acknowledged messianic pattern, to become a political messiah. It was an attempt to under-mine his full acceptance of the will of God and here Peter plays Satan's role. Ironically, the 'Rock' (v 18) has become a 'stumbling-block' (v 23).

Matthew (vv 24-28) has the Lord broaden out a particular occur-rence to apply to all true discipleship of Christ. This following after, through suffering, to the resurrection is not optional – it is a matter of life and death. To accept is to be endowed with the faith of Peter; to refuse is to obstruct God's path as Peter tries to do. To believe is to fall in behind the Lord. To live for God is to trace in one's own life the life of Christ. The cross is actual and symbolic: actual because it stood on Calvary, symbolic because it represents the sufferings, persecutions, martyrdoms, indifference, moral struggles, loveless-ness which every follower of Christ is bound to meet. Jeremiah is not alone in feeling the oppression and constraint of God's call. Every disciple of Christ has in one's own way to face it.

Peter and the Temple Tax 17:24-27

The passage Mt 17:1-23 follows Mk 9:2-32 closely. For Matthew, the transfiguration (Mt 17:1-13), as an anticipation of resurrection and parousia, may be regarded as a confirmation of Peter's confession of Jesus as Son of God (16:16). He has softened the portrayal of Peter and the disciples. There is no trace of the 'he did not know what to say, for they were exceedingly afraid' of Mk 9:6. After the healing of the epileptic boy and the second prediction of the passion (Mt 17:14-23) comes an episode proper to Matthew (17:24-27).

The temple tax (a half-shekel) for the upkeep of the temple was levied on all adult Jewish males. After 70 AD the Romans converted it into a tax for the support of the temple of Jupiter in Rome. When asked if Jesus paid the temple tax the impetuous Peter answered with a confident,Yes. As usual, Jesus gently deflated him. He pointed out that, if the children of kings are exempt from the payment of taxes so, a fortiori, the Son of God is surely not obliged to pay towards the upkeep of his Father's house. For that matter, the disciples, also, as children of the kingdom, are exempt. The passage would seem to come from the early days of Matthew's community. If Jesus' disciples were to refuse to pay the temple tax they would no longer be regarded as Jews – not something they wanted. In that case, 'so that we do not give offense to them' (fellow Jews), the tax should be paid. They would not be compromised. After 70 AD payment of the tax avoided trouble with the Romans. Pragmatism – of course. Only fanatics make an issue of the unimportant. In v 27 we seem to have an instance of a parable turning into a miracle story.

SERMON ON THE CHURCH CH 18

True Greatness 18:1-7

Where Mark (9:33-37) sees a lesson on the dignity of service, Matthew sees a lesson on spiritual childlikeness. We are already on the road to ecclesiasticism with a 'hierarchy' and a 'simple faithful'. Matthew omits Mark's lively action parable (Mk 9:36) but makes the same point. There is no place for degrees of greatness among disciples of Jesus: the least disciple of Jesus has greatness. Whoever receives a child for the sake of Jesus receives Jesus and, in turn, receives the God who sent him. The greatness that comes from belonging to Jesus, from being his disciple, can be enjoyed by a child. Jesus is not establishing the authority of his disciples over others but is pointing out the greatness of discipleship – there is no greater dignity. It follows that ecclesiastical office is, above all, a *service*. This is seen more closely in Mk 8:35 – 'Whoever wants to be first must be last of all and servant of all.' There is no 'first' in the reign of God. Jesus leaves little space for ambition; he leaves no room for the exercise of power.

'These little ones who believe in me': the humblest members of a christian community. 'Put a stumbling block' – a warning on the grievousness of the sin of those who lead simple Christians astray by callously shaking their faith – and here rightwingers are gravely at fault as they propose a merciless God. 'A great millstone', literally, a 'donkey millstone', that is, a millstone turned by a donkey in contrast to the smaller millstone worked by a woman (see Mt 24:41). Death by drowning was a Roman punishment and was particularly repugnant to Jews. The warning, then, is very sharp.

The two logia (vv 8, 9), linked by the catchword *skandalizó*, treat of scandal, not, however, in terms of those who place a stumbling block before others, but in reference to whatever in oneself can cause one to stumble and fall into sin. There is no question, obviously, of actual mutilation, but the vivid Semitic idiom enjoins, in the starkest terms, the costliest sacrifice. The 'Gehenna (hell) of fire': originally, Gehenna – the valley of the son of Hinnom – was a ravine south of Jerusalem where infants were sacrificed to Moloch (Jer 7:31; 10:5-6; 39:35). It was desecrated by Josiah (2 Kgs 23:20) and was henceforth used as a dump for offal and refuse. Jeremiah warned that there the faithless ones of Israel would be destroyed by fire. As a site of ill-omen, it came to symbolise the place of final punishment (see 4 Ezra 7:36; Enoch 27:2). The 'hell of fire': only crass literalism could have led to the later notion of hell as a place of fiery torment. And to a God who condemns sinners to hell: blasphemy by any decent standard.

The Lost Sheep 18:10-14

In Lk 15:4-7 the parable of the lost sheep is an explicit answer to the murmuring of the Pharisees and scribes: 'This fellow welcomes sinners and eats with them.' The same parable occurs in Matthew. Here it is no longer addressed to opponents of the Good News but to disciples. The discourse of which it forms part begins: 'It is not the will of your Father in heaven that one of these little ones should be lost' (18:14). Even if the application were no longer clear the context quite clinches the issue for the warning not to despise one of the least (v 10) and the admonition regarding fraternal/sisterly correction (vv 15-17) leave no doubt about the interpretation of v 14: It is God's will that you go after the erring brother or sister, the weak and helpless one, as earnestly as the shepherd of the parable sought out the lost sheep. It may be that Luke has preserved the original setting of the parable: Jesus' defence of the charge that he was 'friend of sinners'. When one thinks about it, what more appropriate designation of the Son of God, Son of a God who, outrageously, when one reads the Old Testament aright, has a preferential option for sinners. The change of audience in Matthew is readily explained. Early Christians sought in this, as in other parables, a message that met their needs and they took it as applying to themselves. In acting so they had not forced its message. The Lost Sheep was spoken to justify the concern shown by Jesus for sinners and outcasts. The Christian, to be like the Master, should manifest solicitude for the erring brother or sister. There is, simply, a shift of emphasis: an apologetic parable has taken on a hortatory thrust.

Correction 18:15-20

This passage has to do with brotherly/sisterly correction. To be properly evaluated it needs to be read in the context of a chapter which declares the greatness of a childlike sense of littleness (vv 1-5), insists on loving care of the weak members of Christian community (vv 6-14), and is certain that the Christian word, first and last, must be forgiveness (vv 21- 35). In this setting the seemingly harsh demand of excommunication (v 17) appears in a *Christian* light.

The 'brother or sister' contemplated in our passage is not the 'little one' of v 6 nor the weak, candid sinner of v 21. It is one who may prove intransigent. What is important is that Matthew outlines a precisely articulated procedure, a procedure inspired by the Old Testament but which takes on a distinctively Christian flavour. Clearly he has Lev 19:17-18 and Deut 19:15 firmly in mind.

The first point Matthew makes is that within a Christian community one does not *start* by 'passing the buck', by planting the problem straight on the leader's desk. The proper procedure is *privately* to approach the erring brother or sister. If the intervention succeeds that is the end of the matter, and one has the joy of winning over a

brother or sister. If another attempt becomes necessary it it still a
private matter involving only two or three community members
(see Deut 9:15). If this fails, only then is the whole community to
take up, formally, the case of an obstinate sinner. From first to last it
is a *community* concern. And, if has to come to it, it is the community
that excommunicates.

In the Judaism of Jesus' day 'Gentile' was a pagan outsider and 'tax-
collector' a traitor. Matthew's largely Jewish-Christian community
would have inherited such characterisation but would have gone
on to regard 'Gentile' as the non-Christian and 'tax-collector' as one
who can no longer be called Christian. The community, vulnerably
human as it is (see 1 Cor 5:6), must protect itself against threat from
within as well as from without. All the while, a prime concern must
be the (eternal) welfare of the sinner. If the sinner repents – and that is
the hope – then forgiveness must be warm and without limit or condition (Mt 18:21-22). Each and every Christian, because he or she has
encountered a forgiving Father, would be eager to forgive (18:23-25).

In their present context vv 18-20 mean that the verdict of the community (if arrived at a truly Christian way) will be ratified by God.
Originally, it is clear that these sayings had to do with *prayer*. And
there is the assurance that where Christians (even two or three)
gather in Jesus' name, he is with them – he is Emmanuel, God-with-
us (see 1:23; 28:20). And surely there is the admonition that the
grave matter of discipling a brother or sister is never a question of
'throwing the book' at one. It has to be a *prayerful* decision.
Otherwise, while it may stand as a decision, it will not stand as a
Christian deed.

Forgiveness 18:21-35

Just as ben Sirach (Sir 28:2-4) regards the forgiveness of our neighbour as crucially important for right human conduct (Sir 28:2-4), so
Matthew underlines its significance for the early church. This passage forms the conclusion of his 'community discourse'. Though he
had to face the uncomfortable fact that an unrepentant brother or
sister might have to be excluded from the community (18:15-20) he
wants to ensure that his word on relationships within the community will end on the resounding note of forgiveness.

While Luke (17:4) also gives the first saying about forgiveness, Matthew adds special importance to it in three ways: by putting the question in the mouth of Peter, leader of the Christian community; by increasing the number of times from seven (already the perfect number signifying 'any number of times') to seventy-seven (or seventy times seven) – an unlimited number of times; by adding the parable, as he likes to do at the end of a discourse to drive the point home.

The disparity between the two sums mentioned in the parable is gigantic – ten thousand talents is an unimaginable sum. A debt impossible of repayment is written off, casually, by the king, and the man is not even sacked. It is quite the situation one finds in Lk 15:11-24. Yet, one who had been shown such mercy cannot find it in his heart to remit a paltry debt. Not only that: he will not even give his fellow-servant – his social equal – reasonable time and opportunity to repay. The king who had been moved with 'pity' (v 27) is now 'angry' (v 34).

The parable is a thinly-veiled allegory. The 'servant' is the sinner; his situation is hopeless. The 'king' is a merciful God who freely and lovingly forgives any sin. Luke has painted the warmer picture of prodigal Father and wayward child (15:11-24). The reality is the same in either case. Like the younger son in the Lucan parable this man, too, is forgiven with no strings attached. Faced with a cry of desperation the forgiving God was moved with pity (Mt 18:27). But when the recipient of such forgiveness cannot find it in his heart to be merciful the Master is angry (18:33). Response to God's gracious forgiveness cannot be payment of a debt that is already fully remitted. It is, instead, warm thanksgiving for the blessing of such forgiving love. And the story in Matthew underlines again that sin, as God regards it, is man's inhumanity to man (even more sadly, man's inhumanity to woman) whatever shape that may take. Our abuse of others (and of ourselves) is an affront to the loving Father who counts us as his children. Jesus clearly understood this because he knew his Father. A corollary. Jesus asks us, frail humans, to be forgiving, without limit. He dares to ask the impossible because he knew that his God is an Abba whose forgiveness literally knows no limit.

CHAPTER 8

Towards the Passion 19-23

Come, you that are blessed by my Father (Mt 25:34)

NARRATIVE: MOUNTING OPPOSITION 19-23

What Jesus meant by God's reign – the rule of God – has been firmly caught by the author of the letter to Titus: 'When the goodness and loving kindness of God our Saviour appeared, he saves us, not because of any works of righteousness that we had done, but according to his mercy' (Titus 3:4-5). The God of Jesus is a God who has supreme concern for people. His lordship points to an ideal, God-willed relationship between God and humankind. Jesus lived and died for the establishment of that rule. He ached for men and women to discover the love of God for humankind and give substance to the wonder of the discovery through loving concern for one another. That love would involve sacrifice and suffering. It meant sacrifice and suffering for Jesus. Opposition to him is visible throughout the gospel. Now it becomes more bitter and more threatening. Still, Jesus' message, despite an increased note of warning, continues to be one of hope and promise. One seriously suspects that the negative note issues not from Jesus but from a Matthew faced with community problems. Happily, there are are still some who do believe that Jesus revealed the Abba, the wondrous Hebrew God of *infinite* love. The narrative in Mt 19-23 is interspersed by parables. In keeping with the emphasis of this book on Jesus as teacher, we will concentrate on these parables.

Labourers in the Vineyard 20:1-16

A major difficulty in interpreting the parables of Jesus is that we can never be sure when, where and in what circumstances Jesus spoke a parable. The setting provided by an evangelist usually reflects his own concern. It is evident that Matthew intends the parable of the labourers in the vineyard to be understood in close connection with

Jesus' promise of reward to his disciples (19:27-30). It is just as clear that the parable does not fit smoothly into that context. For Jesus, the parable surely has to do with God's generosity which transcends human standards.

The saying, 'So the last will be first and the first last' (v 16) is certainly not the conclusion of the original parable – it is an independent and floating *logion* (see 19:30; Mk 10:31; Lk 13:30). We can even see why it was added in Matthew. Verses 8b, 'Call the labourers and give them their pay, beginning with the last and then going to the first', seemed to represent a reversal of rank that would take place at the judgment and the saying would appear to be perfectly in place. But it is so only at first sight because the wage is still the same in each case. Besides, v 8b may be rendered quite accurately: 'Pay them their wages, including the last as well as the first.'

The parable, then, originally ended at v 15, and the key to it is the last phrase of the verse: 'because I am generous'. It is this goodness that explains the apparently capricious conduct of the householder. For, indeed, at first sight, it does seem unfair that all the workers were to receive the same wage. But when we understand his motive we judge his conduct very differently. A denarius represented a day's wage, just enough to support a family; anything less, and especially payment for a single hour, would be inadequate. It is because he had pity on them that the owner called them to his vineyard in the first place and it is because he has pity on them that he pays them all a full wage. There is nothing arbitrary in his conduct – it is the action of a man who is full of compassion for the poor. So, too, does God act, for God is all goodness and mercy. This is the message of the parable.

But if we look at it again we shall see that it is two-pronged, that it is made up of two episodes. First we have the hiring of the labourers and instruction about their payment (vv 1-8), and then follows the indignation of the recipients who feel themselves cheated (vv 9-15). It is characteristic of such parables that the emphasis falls on the second part. Because that is so here, we should realise that the parable is aimed at people who resemble the murmurers. The fact is: God is not 'fair!' The parable shows what God is like, full of compassion for the poor. It points out how wrong-headed it is to be scandalised by his great goodness. Matthew is hitting at some 'begrudgers' within his community. God's prodigal goodness is an affront to human level-headedness. God's love of sinners is insult to the pious.

The Two Sons 21:28-32

Throughout the gospel Matthew has been making the point that by rejecting and killing the Son, Israel brought about its own rejection. The Gentiles have received the kingdom Israel has forfeited. Our parable of the two sons (proper to Matthew) is explicitly directed against the leaders of the Jews and Jesus puts their own condemnation in the mouths of his accusers (v 30-31). As so often, the vineyard (following Isaiah 5) stands for Israel, God's chosen people, and the contrast is made between the seemingly obedient sons of the father, the 'righteous' Jews, and those whom Jesus' hearers regarded as contemptible outcasts. On the face of it they refuse what is required of them because they do not observe the law, but they in fact please God more by their openness and love. The point of the parable is that the leaders of the Jews who have promised to work for God, but have failed to do so, will be rejected. 'I go, sir' (v 30) – 'sir' is *kyrie* or 'Lord'. The son is one who says, 'Lord, Lord' but does not do the will of the Father (7:21). Others who have said 'No' to God at first (the tax collectors and the prostitutes, for example) but have afterwards repented and done his will, are received into God's kingdom. The reaction of the first son is a key factor in the parable: he 'changed his mind' – thought better of his initial refusal. What we profess to believe has no value if it is not translated into active obedience (see 7:21-27). This warning is addressed to 'religious' people in every age.

The Evil Tenants 21:33-43

The motifs of vineyard and son link this parable to the preceding one (21:28-32). Together with 21:1-14 it forms a series of three parables illustrating Israel's leaders refusal of the kingdom and thus Israel's threatened loss of privilege as God's chosen people. The background to this parable is clearly Is 5:1-7. Only, there is a distinction between 'vineyard' and 'tenants.' The 'householder's' contention is not with the vineyard (that is, Israel) but with the tenants (that is, Israel's leaders). In fact this parable, along with the other two, is addressed to 'the chief priests and elders of the people' (21: 23, 28, 45; 22:1). It is an allegorical parable depicting Israel's doleful history and the failure of the leaders.

The landowner is God. The vineyard is Israel. The wicked tenants are the religious leaders of Israel. The servants are the prophets. The son is Jesus. The son's death is his crucifixion outside Jerusalem (see Heb 13:13-14). The reference (in v 42) to Ps 118:22-23 pinpoints Jesus' triumph in his resurrection, not merely in spite of but precisely because of his rejection by contemporary Jewish leaders. Unwittingly, the tenants were right when they said: 'This is the heir, come let us kill him and get his inheritance' (v 38). For, para-doxically, it was only by being rejected by people and being chosen by God that Jesus became the saviour not alone of the nations but also of Israel.

This parable also functions as a theological explanation of the death of Jesus. Jesus was 'delivered up' to death – he was 'handed over according to the definite plan and foreknowledge of God' (Acts 2:22). What does this mean? The parable gives the answer. The Son knew the Father and came to do his will. His life was not laid down in answer to divine need. It was laid down in answer to divine love. Father and Son were prepared to go to any length to save us humans from ourselves. 'Surely, they will respect my Son!' The death of Jesus was, ultimately, sacrifice made by the Father. Paul had got it right: 'He who did not withhold his own Son, but gave him up for all of us, will he not with him also give us everything else?' (Rom 8:32).

Royal Wedding Feast 22:1-14

Drawing their inspiration from Is 25:6-10 (among other passages) Jesus' contemporaries envisaged the arrival of God's reign in terms of a banquet, an eschatological celebration. Jesus addressed his parable of the wedding feast (see Rev 19:9) to those people (in the present context, the chief priests and leaders of the people) who consider that, belonging to Israel, they have no need to reply to the invitation in order to enter the banquet of the kingdom – they have reserved places. Emphasis is on the invitation and its acceptance or rejection. Like the vineyard (Mt 21:28-32, 33-43) the banquet is a metaphor. If the former image brings out the 'fruit-bearing' - aspect of the kingdom, the latter emphasises both its joy and the need to respond to God's call when he invites people to enter. In reaction to rejection of his invitation 'the king sent his troops, destroyed those murderers, and burned their city' (v 7). The reference is to the destruction of Jerusalem in 70 AD. Matthew echoes an early Christian interpretation of the event: it happened because some in Israel rejected the invitation to the kingdom and maltreated the messengers – especially Jesus. Yet again that sad human penchant for depicting God as, somehow, vindictive. The 'slaves' of vv 8-10 are Christian apostles whose preaching gathers together all and sundry. The 'wedding hall' of v 10 is the church, the community of those who have hearkened to the good news.

Matthew's final scene (vv 11-13) is really a separate parable added to the first. (This explains the incongruity that people dragged in off the street [v 10] are blamed for not being properly dressed for a wedding [v 12]). It is Matthew's warning to the church. The church is held together neither by family ties nor by an external structure, but by the active, personal and continual response to God's word. The response is the work of a lifetime. The 'wedding robe' of v 11-12 is a symbol of this response, that is, of a life lived in conformity with God's word as it has been revealed in Christ. The condemnation of v 13 is a warning to Christians that they, too, like the religious leaders of Israel, can fail to answer God's invitation. The observation of v 14 (which does not really fit vv 1-10 or 11-13) does suit Matthew's general intention, a reminder of the need to respond to God's call. God's invitation is to all ('many') but only those who truly respond will become the chosen, the elect. Mere membership of the church is not enough. Response is in doing the will of the Father (7:21). Happily, God and the Son are always more gracious than those who speak in their name.

Attempted Entrapment 22:15-40

Matthew 22:15-21 is the first of three attempts (see 22:23-33, 34-40) on the part of Jesus' adversaries 'to entrap him in what he said'. The present ruse is obvious. By and large the Pharisees were anti-Roman while the Herodians (supporters of the dynasty of Herod) were pro-Roman. The question of the legitimacy of paying taxes to Rome was a lively one for Jesus' contemporaries. Jesus is faced with a dilemma: 'Is it lawful to pay … or not?' If he were to answer 'yes' he would lose the esteem of the people and be discredited as a traitor to the Jewish cause of independence from Rome. If he were to answer 'no' he could be denounced as fomenting rebellion – Rome regarded refusal to pay taxes as tantamount to rebellion.

Jesus cleverly evaded the trap by asking his questioners for a denarius, the Roman coin used to pay the poll- tax (the tax in question here). They promptly produced one. He had scored a point: they, ostensibly so concerned about the implication of the tax, thereby conceded that they carried and used Caesar's money. By using Caesar's money, he implied, they tacitly accepted his imperial system and should be prepared to pay his taxes. Give back to him what is his: 'Give therefore to the emperor the things that are the emperor's' Jesus went on to declare: 'and to God the things that are God's' He can hardly mean that there are some things that belong to Caesar and others which belong to God, as if reality were divisible into 'secular' and 'sacred.' What he means is that an obligation to Caesar stands under and is judged by a paramount obligation to acknowledge the sovereignty of the supreme Sovereign.

This classic pronouncement-story – it manifestly builds up to the pronouncement, the punch-line, of v 21 – offers no neat solution to the question of Church-State relations. The legitimate state has rights and the good citizen will respect them. For the Christian there may come a time when one must hearken to the supreme Sovereign rather than to the state. Jesus has given a principle but, like so much of his teaching, it has to be lived out in situations that are not at all clear. Christians, and the church, must, so often, be content to live with uncertainty.

In 22 23-33 the Sadducees poured ridicule on the 'new-fangled' doctrine of the resurrection of the body. Jesus pointed out that they were mistaken on two counts: in their interpretation of the Pentateuch and in their failure to understand the power of God who is capable of achieving something beyond human imagining and, in particular, make resurrection life something different from

and higher than life in this world. Jesus, in fact, presented the current more sophisticated (as opposed to the popular) notion of the
resurrection. Paul's teaching in 1 Cor 15:35-50 is a good formulation
of the same view.

In Mt 22:34-40 there is a third attempt to 'entrap Jesus in what he
said' (22:15). By rabbinical count, the 'law' comprised 613 commandments, thus providing the scribes with the question about the
greatest commandment. The aim of the question addressed to Jesus
was to have him commit himself on a much-debated topic and thus
make it possible for the 'crowds' (21:46) to be divided about him.
Evading the trap, Jesus pinpointed as the greatest commandment
what is not, strictly speaking, a commandment at all but rather the
'soul' of all the commandments: the love of God.

In reply to his questioner Jesus quoted Deuteronomy 6:4-5, the
heart of the *Shema*, a prayer recited, morning and evening, by observant Jews. But Jesus did not stop there. He went on to make this
'abstract' commandment very concrete and practical by quoting
also Lev 19-18: 'you shall love your neighbour as yourself.' What is
new is not the bringing of these commandments together but the
making them of equal weight and importance. What is more, Jesus
declared (v 40) that all the laws of the Old Testament and all the
preaching of the prophets – the whole of God's revelation – 'hang
upon' these two commandments as upon a double peg. Jesus did
not spell out the relationship between the two commandments. He
left if for a Paul (Rom 13:8-10) and a John (Jn 13:34) to show that, in
fact, they are not two commandments but one: the love of God in
the love of one's neighbour.

Style of Authority 23:1-12

Conflict between the Jewish authorities and Jesus is well documented
in the gospels. But Matthew 23 is something special. As it stands, it
is an indictment of Pharisaic Judaism painfully reflecting the bitter
estrangement of church and synagogue towards the close of the
first century AD. What we have here is the thoroughgoing rejection
of Pharisaic Judaism by Matthew and his community. This
accounts for the disturbing harshness of the Matthean Jesus' tirade.
It should be recalled that the earliest Matthean community saw

itself as an exclusive reform movement within Judaism and regarded itself as more observant than the Pharisees. This explains the otherwise surprising statement: 'The scribes and the Pharisees sit on Moses' seat, so practice and observe what they tell you but not what they do' (23:2-3). It is an echo from that first period when the Matthean group saw itself as going beyond Pharisaism in meticulous observance of Torah. At the later stage it could be read as a barb aimed at *Christian* leaders guilty of hypocrisy. Indeed, the passage 23:1-2 does envisage Christian leaders.

The point Matthew makes in this passage is that the Christian leaders of his community are to avoid the rabbinic style. After nearly two millennia of ecclesiastical practice it makes sad reading. We are at once faced with the difficulty that in vv 2-3 the Matthean Jesus acknowledges the legitimacy of Pharisaic teaching authority and urges compliance with *whatever* the Pharisees teach and command. Elsewhere, Matthew has firmly rejected Pharisaic teaching (15:1-20; 16:1-12) and, in our chapter, he rejects their practices in vv 5-10 and their teaching in vv 16-20. As it stands, chapter 23 is an indictment of Pharisaic Judaism painfully reflecting the bitter estrangement of church and synagogue towards the end of the first century AD. Yet, Matthew instances scribes and Pharisees as the negative side of Christian leadership.

The Pharisees are criticised because their interpretation of the law takes little or no account of human frailty and tends to be more severe than humane (v 4). They are people who make custom their dictator, vanity and ostentation their life-style. Showing off, parading piety, enjoying the limelight, insisting upon places of honour – these are forms of play-acting, incredible performances in the name of religion (vv 5-7). How painfully representative of ecclesiastical style, even to our day. Happily, it is taking something of a beating. But is there really any justification for silly titles and bizarre garb. Matthew's word to leaders in his community is: you must remember that you are *servants* of the community. You must avoid the titles 'rabbi', 'father', 'teacher.' The title Rabbi – literally, 'my great one' – would sit incongruously on one who is 'slave' of the community. Nor is any to be addressed as 'teacher' – practically the same as 'rabbi'. Already, by Matthew's day, religious leaders were seek-

ing to be 'real' leaders!. True religion as taught and exemplified by
Jesus is a family-of-God affair, characterised by simplicity, affec-
tion, brother/sisterhood (vv 8-12). What he was insisting on – and
this is what his followers were meant to be aware of – was that the
teacher is the minister and servant of God's word to the people.
There is only one Father, God, and all people are brothers and sisters. There ought not be an insistence on privilege and on exercise
of power that distorts this relationship.

Seven Woes 23:13-36

The seven woes might be paraphrased:

Woe to you scribes and Pharisees; you are hypocrites: externally
strict observers of the law; inwardly corrupt. Woe to you:

> because you shut the door of the kingdom of heaven and pre-
> vent people from entering.

> because you travel over sea and land to win one convert – and
> then make him a bigger hypocrite than yourselves.

> because you say: to swear by the Temple gold is binding – not an
> oath by the Temple! To swear by the gift on the altar is binding –
> not an oath by the altar! Surely, the altar is greater than the gift,
> the Temple greater than its gold! And one who swears by the
> Temple is swearing by the One who dwells there.

> because you tithe the most insignificant of garden herbs – and
> ignore the real matters of the Law: justice, mercy, faith. You
> legalists: straining out gnats and gulping a camel!

> because you cleanse the outside of cup and dish, and leave the
> inside full of robbery and self-indulgence – very images of your-
> selves!

> because you are like whitewashed tombs: outwardly upright;
> inside full of hypocrisy and crime.

> because you venerate the martyred prophets – you sons of their
> murderers! Finish off what your fathers began – by murdering
> the Son of Man!

The holy city had rejected the eschatological – the last – prophet
(23:37-39). There is no recovery from this rejection – there will be no
other prophet. The people of Israel will encounter their rejected

Messiah next time on the day of judgment. Then they will recognise him – but too late. Israel had had its chance and had failed. In view of the 'woes' and the awesome declaration of 27:25 (seen as fulfilment of the word of 23:35-36) one must be alert to the whole of the New Testament message and, above all, sensitive to the startlingly new teaching of Jesus. Not only later Christians, but New Testament Christians, too, found it hard, or impossible to live up to his ideal. His challenge still rings out to all who will listen. The God of Jesus is ever the Father of infinite love, of unbounded forgiveness.

JUDGMENT SERMON 24-25

When Matthew wrote his gospel (around 90 AD) the Jerusalem temple had long been destroyed (in 70 AD). If he nevertheless gives a prediction of its end and an outline of the sufferings of the Jewish war (66-70 AD) it is because he hopes that he can thereby help Christians to respond adequately to their present difficulties. The first part of Matthew's eschatological discourse (24:1-36) follows Mark 13 very closely – though with typical modifications. Jesus had spoken a word against the temple in 23:38. Now as he leaves it he speaks plainly of its total destruction (24:1-2). Then, seated on the Mount of Olives, he turns to the group of disciples.

The topic of interest in their question (24:3) is not the end of the temple but the time of the Lord's parousia and the end of the world. Jesus does not answer the question directly; instead he starts to warn of the 'birth pangs' – a traditional term to express the view that the messianic age would come to birth amidst a period of woes. It will be a time of false prophets and pseudo-messianic claimants. War and famine denote the Jewish war but, in apocalyptic style, point beyond to the cosmic events to come.

The next stage figures in vv 9-14 – the tribulation of the church: suffering coming from without and from within. A hostile world will *deliver up* the disciples to death: Christians will be hated and persecuted because of the *name* – the person – of Jesus. More dreadful is the prospect of betrayal and apostasy fostered by mischief-making prophets. All is not lost; some will endure faithfully to the end and win salvation. They are those who, in face of troubles from within and from without, will steadfastly proclaim 'the good news of the Kingdom', the good news of the triumphant coming of God's reign. Only with this universal proclamation of the Gospel will the end be at hand.

False messianic claimants and false prophets must have been a bother for Matthew's church because they emerge again to heighten the alarming picture of the last days (24:23-28). These false prophets may make appeal to the Christ of their own desire and imagining but there is the comfort that they will not succeed in leading astray faithful Christians. There will be challenges, too, from messianic and esoteric circles outside the Christian body. But when the Son of man comes it will be as suddenly and as visibly as a bolt of lightning. Thus any who claim secret knowledge of the time of his coming must not be listened to.

The question of 24:3 is answered: the parousia of the Son of man and the close of the age will follow immediately on the great tribulation (24:29-31). The cosmic signs which accompany the parousia are part and parcel of Jewish apocalyptic descriptions of the Day of the Lord. The Son of man will come in glory, riding triumphantly on the clouds of heaven. With supreme authority, but with graciousness, the Son of man will gather *his* elect – they belong to him. This gathering will be the last task of *his* angels, those 'ministering spirits, sent out to serve those who are to inherit salvation' (Heb 1:14).

Watchfulness 24:36-25:46

The tone of the second part of the discourse (24:36-25:46) is emphatically that of moral exhortation. It opens with three short parables on vigilance (24:36-44). Some Christians were overeager for the parousia (24:36) while others were indifferent to it or were leading lives of careless unreadiness. They are warned that judgment is imminent. A carefree business-as-usual attitude was typical of the contemporaries of Noah; what they were doing was not wrong in itself but they had no thought of God. The end was sudden and unexpected and their heedlessness left them unprepared. People will be judged as individuals and not in batches (24:40-41). Two men (or two women) will not necessarily share the same judgment simply because they work at the same occupation. One will be taken, the other left (as one was taken aboard the ark, for salvation, another left behind, for destruction). Warning of the return of Jesus like a *thief* in the night prepares for the moral: 'You must be prepared in the same way.' The theme of the future soft-footing into the present like a burglar is present elsewhere in the New Testament (1 Thess 5:2,4; 2 Pet 3:10). The only preparation possible, the only preparation necessary, is our constant care to live in the light and love of the Lord made man for us. When Matthew wrote his gospel, the old Israel was already destroyed. This did not mean that the church can now forget about judgment. But judgment will not be as dramatic as in the majestic scene of Matthew 25. The second coming is a powerful statement of the completeness of God's saving plan for humankind. Alertness is all the more emphasised because this evangelist has a developed consciousness of the length of time which must elapse before the 'coming'. Hence the warnings to the lukewarm and the demand for watchfulness.

The three short parables of watchfulness are followed by three longer ones. The first (24:45-51) is aimed specifically at church leaders. They are urged to be prudent and faithful in their caring for the community. The temptation is that the leader who lacks a sense of urgency will forget that he is a servant and begin to lord it over others. For Matthew the 'hypocrites' are the Jewish leaders. The unfaithful Christian leader is no better than they and will come under a like condemnation.

The parable of the ten maidens is proper to Matthew (25:1-13). The introductory formula does not, of course, mean that the kingdom be directly compared to ten maidens. It is shorthand for: 'It is the case with the kingdom of heaven as with ten maidens…' The final coming of the kingdom may be likened to the whole situation about to be described.

It would seem that the ten girls wait at the bridegroom's house to greet, formally, the bridegroom when he comes with his bride after a night-time wedding. The cry, 'Lord, Lord' of the foolish ones (v 11) echoes the 'Lord, Lord' of 7:21 – of those who are not doers of the word. And the reply of 'the Lord' in each case is the same: 'I never knew you' (7:23); 'I do not know you' (25:12). The parable stresses constant watchfulness (even though all the girls fall asleep for a time, even those who are admitted to the wedding feast!) In a broader sense, it points to the seriousness of our relationship with God. This is something each person must possess for oneself; nobody else can fashion it for one. It is something each one must work at and live during one's lifetime; one cannot borrow it at the last moment. It is of vital importance because it is really a statement of how one sees oneself and the meaning of one's life.

The Talents 25:14-30

In 25:1-13 Matthew had dealt with the delay of the parousia (a parousia that will happen in its time, 24:48-51). Now he goes on to explain what it means to be watchful or ready during the delay. It is to be faithful to the Lord's instructions and to carry them out, energetically, with all our God-given ability. We are not to sit back, arms folded, quietly waiting for the Lord. The time of waiting is meant to be filled by our deeds of love.

The 'talent' entrusted to the servants is the largest currency unit of the time. (Precisely because of this parable the word 'talent' has taken on its familiar metaphorical meaning). The first two servants by industrious trading doubled the respective amounts received. The third, a man afflicted with 'prudence', carefully hid his money. With his 'after a long time' (v 19) Matthew denotes the delay of the parousia. The Lord ('master' is *ho kyrios*) returned and held a reckoning. The first two servants are congratulated and rewarded for their enterprise and fidelity. The reward of faithful and profitable service is greater responsibility and an acceptance into a more intimate relationship with the Lord. Though their responsibility had been unequal (five talents and two talents) their reward is the same (vv 21, 23): what matters is wholehearted commitment, not accomplishment.

The third servant receives blame and condemnation – because he had done nothing. He had been too 'prudent' to take a risk. Punishment is for disuse rather than abuse of what had been entrusted. The servant's characterisation of the Master as 'a harsh man' betrays his manner of imaging God (quite like that of the elder son of Luke's parable: 'all these years I have been working like a slave for you, and I have never disobeyed your command' – Lk 15:29). One who images God so will strive to live within 'safe' legal parameters, will take no risk. The others had the confidence and the freedom to 'trade' (vv 16-17).

Matthew would seem to be warning Christian leaders who portrayed God as an exacting taskmaster to the detriment of his loving Parenthood. The upshot is that the inactive servant loses everything. Likely, v 29 was originally a cynical proverb to the effect that the rich get richer and the poor poorer. In its present context it refers to human response to God's gift. One who commits oneself will receive generously; one who is ungenerous and selfish will end up losing what little one has. The warning is clear: a Christian who will not 'do' one's faith must face a bitter reckoning.

The Judgment 25:31-46

This is Matthew's great scene of the Last Judgment. In it the Son of Man is emphatically a King who sits in judgment. Perhaps largely through the influence of this passage the image of Christ as Judge has had a profound impact on Christian tradition – an unhappy impact. This image of Christ is far from being the dominant one in the New Testament. And, even in our passage, when one looks closely, it will be seen that judgment is 'auto-judgment': we judge ourselves by our omissions or our deeds. It is not so surprising that there has been concern with the King and the Judge: that drew attention from a disturbing factor. Properly understood, the passage is subversive of ecclesiastical system; it is a denial of the label 'Christian' to any church not characterised by loving concern for the poor. It underlines the fact that if Christ is King, his kingdom, his manner of kingship, is not of this world (see Jn 18:36).

In the parables of chapters 24-25 Matthew had summoned to watchfulness, to readiness, to faithfulness. Now, in 25:31-46 he spells out what it means to be watchful and ready and faithful. It means being able to recognise the Son of Man in all those in need, to be loving towards the Son of Man in those in need, to translate this love into deeds of concern. There is the yardstick and by it one is

measured. On performance of or on neglect of these works of mercy
hang salvation.

Rightly to appreciate this passage one must understand that it is
retrospective. Matthew has in mind how Jesus comported himself –
how he related to people. What Jesus did and said becomes the
standard of judgment. He had come, a human being, into our
human history, to tell us of the Godness of God. Jesus taught and
lived that the reality of God is revealed in the realisation of more
humanity between fellow human beings – giving drink to the
thirsty, feeding the hungry, welcoming the stranger. Matthew's
story of judgment is focused on purely human concerns. But these
are God's concern: 'Come, you blessed of my Father.' The emphasis
is on the needy person, the one in distress. What is at stake in this
last judgment is our attitude towards the little ones, the humble and
the needy. The criterion is not the standard of religion or cult. It is,
starkly: has one helped those in need.

The scene is vivid. Mixed flocks of (white) sheep and (black) goats
were a common sight in Palestine. Here sheep and goats separate
for final blessing or curse. The King of the heavenly kingdom sits in
judgment on his people. The good works of vv 34-36 are the traditional 'corporal works of mercy' and the elect have performed these
works. Their surprise, their amazement, is in being told by the king
that they had been done 'to me'. Astounded, they ask: 'When?…
when?… when?' The answer is Jesus' solemn attestation of his total
identification with the poor and outcast and oppressed. It might
seem, at first sight, that this Matthean scene has nothing specifically
Christian about it. But when we realise that nothing less than the
comportment of Jesus himself is the yardstick of judgment, we can
see how thoroughly Christian it is. And this is so even though it
embraces 'all the nations' – all people without distinction (25:32).

The truth is that the King who is Judge of all is the crucified King
and he is met in every one who suffers. It is because they had failed
to understand Jesus' identification with the suffering that the
'goats' had failed to minister to him and serve him. They had not
loved the poor in concrete deeds of mercy. This Jesus, the crucified
one, is the Son of man who utters judgment – but what kind of judg-

ment is this? He is the one who identifies himself with the lowly –
with all the daughters and sons of men. He is the loving and living
expression of God's concern for humankind. A God bent on
humankind, and nothing short of that, becomes the standard of our
concern for those in need. That is why just this concern is the
criterion of judgment. That is why the words of warning sound so
harshly: 'Depart from me, you cursed.'

Straightway: a problem. Can one, as a Christian, really believe that
the suffering Jesus on the cross who in Luke's passion-story prayed:
'Father, forgive them; for they do not know what they do' (Lk 23:34)
could, as risen Lord, declare in awful judgment: 'Depart from me,
you cursed, into the eternal fire'? Matthew, it seems (25:41) would
have us think so. That such is really his intent becomes incredible
when we understand that the 'they' of Luke's text embraces all who
brought Jesus to death. Jesus prays forgiveness for the obdurate
chief priests and their allies. Luke is suggesting that even perpetra-
tors of evil never really appreciate God's goodness or the strange
wisdom of his purpose. Besides, we should see that seeming irrevo-
cable sentence against what we know of the God of the Old
Testament and the New. He is the wondrously inconsistent God
who 'grieves to his heart' that he had ever made this complicated,
stubborn and treacherous human creature (Gen 6:5-8) – only to
decide to put up with them henceforth (Gen 8:21); she is the God
whose mother-heart recoils at the prospect of losing Ephraim (Hos
11:8); he is the God who desires the salvation of all (1 Tim 2:40); he
is the God who did not spare his own Son (Jn 3:16). Surely Jesus
would have us believe that his God and ours loves us with divine
love that is beyond our human imagining.

Still, what are we to make of Matthew's Last Judgment? We are to
understand it as myth. Myth is a symbolic form of expression
couched in narrative which is not intended to be historical. It deals
with realities which transcend experience – in this case the reality of
definitive encounter with God.

In effect, the 'last judgment' is warning: it primarily relates to one's
conduct in the present. One is challenged to live in such a way that,
should it occur, one would not be caught unawares. We are being

taught how we should prepare for the 'coming' of the Lord, prepared for our meeting with him. The 'last judgment' is taking place in my life here and now. The 'books' are being written. But, has my name 'been written in the book of life since the foundation of the world' (Rev 17:8)? There is the true judgment.

As a closing comment, I like, and have made my own, a provocative word on the Matthean judgment scene:

> I believe – and I say this with some hesitation – that at the last judgment perhaps everyone will stand at the right-hand side of the Son of Man: 'Come all you beloved people, blessed of the Father, for despite all your inhumanity, you once gave a glass of water when I was in need. Come!'[18]

Does that seem outrageous? I do not think so. That man of Nazareth, who went about doing good, who died on a cross because he had espoused the cause of human freedom – he will not have us see God as an inflexible judge. He would have us see the tears of a God who weeps in concert with human woe.

CHAPTER 9

Climax: Passion, Death, Resurrection 26-28

And remember, I am with you always,
to the end of the age (Mt 28:20)

'When Jesus had finished saying all these things' – this phrase concludes each of the Sermons (see 7:28; 11:1; 13:53; 19:1). Now there is a ring of finality. The time of preaching is over; the mission is at an end. In Matthew, Jesus prophesies his Passion: 'You know that after two days the Passover is coming, and the Son of Man will be handed over to be crucified' (26: 2; see Mk 14:1).

Plot, Anointing, Betrayal 26:6-16

The sequel to the priests' plot to arrest Jesus by stealth (vv 3-5) is obviously Judas' betrayal (vv 14-16). The intercalated anointing scene (vv 6-13) is thereby highlighted and is meant to be understood in the context of the framework. The woman is not named, nor are those who object to her action: interest falls on the words of Jesus (vv 10-13). She had performed a good service, more significant than she knew. Anointing for burial was not her intent; it is how Jesus chose to view it. Her gesture, at the opening of the passion, points to the heart of the Good News: salvation through the death of the Saviour. Poignantly, the lovely deed of this unknown woman stands between the deadly intent of the priests and the betrayal of Jesus by a disciple.

PASSION AND DEATH 26:36-27:66

In his Passion Narrative, Matthew has followed Mark quite closely. Both gospels present a Jesus who is abandoned by his followers and who has to face his hour alone. Both have a Jewish trial of Jesus and a Roman trial. The Jewish authorities tried to convict Jesus of planning to destroy the Temple. When he acknowledged that he is the

Messiah, the Son of God, he was accused of blasphemy. The Roman trial centred on Jesus' being the King of the Jews. While Pilate knows that Jesus is a just man, he handed him over to be crucified. Both authorities failed to grant Jesus justice and both maltreated him. There is no friend or supporter by the cross; Jesus was rejected and mocked.

Two prayers frame the journey to the cross. At the beginning, in Gethsemane, Jesus prayed to his Abba-Father to let the cup pass from him. At the end, on Golgotha, he prayed to 'my God', asking why he has been forsaken. He died with an anguished cry, seemingly wholly defeated. If Jesus' prayer had not gone unanswered, his God had not been absent at all.

> In their Passion Narrative Mark/Matthew dramatise how difficult it is for Jesus to go through his crucifixion and how he is clearly recognised as belonging to God only after he has suffered to the full. This is meant both as a graphic warning and a consolation to the readers of these Gospels. If the Master found it difficult, if the closest disciples all failed to follow Jesus in bearing the cross, the readers too will find it difficult and will flee. Yet the God who vindicated Jesus, though at times seeming to have forsaken them, will ultimately be their vindicator as well when their final hour has come and their Golgotha looms before them, if like them they have the courage to say 'Let us go.'[19]

While the Passion Narratives of Mark and Matthew are remarkably close there are still significant differences. Here we will concentrate on the distinctive elements of the Matthean narrative.[20]

Special Matthean Passion Material
1. The Death of Judas 27:3-10
2. The Dream of Pilate's Wife 27:19
3. Pilate Washes His Hands 27:24-25
4. A Popular Poetic Quatrain 27:51b-53
5. The Guard-at-the-Tomb 27:62-66; 28:2-4, 11-15.

Brown finds in the special material Matthew has grouped around the birth and death of Jesus a consistency that points to a source – a 'popular' source. He discerns in this special material a strongly anti-Jewish character. The Jewish authorities seem notably malevolent. Even the Jewish crowd is emphatically antagonistic. The Jewish nation has brought upon itself the divine punishment which in the Jewish Christian view (and Matthew is a Jewish Christian gospel) found expression in the destruction of Jerusalem and its Temple. 'Such broad polemics against "the Jews" … go beyond what is found in the body of Matthew's Gospel. In my opinion they reflect the unnuanced, prejudiced theological judgments found among the ordinary people who are the source of the stories that make up the Matthean special material.'[21]

The major Matthean difference from Mark is the introduction of responsibility for the death of Jesus. In Old Testament terms it is presented as guilt of the blood of an innocent person wrongfully condemned to death. This emerges in scenes peculiar to Matthew. Judas tries to shake off his responsibility; the chief priests seek to get rid of the 'blood money'; Pilate's wife warns him to extricate himself from his involvement with this just man; Pilate washes his hands. No attempt succeeds; all are tainted by their part in shedding innocent blood.

Modifications

In a lead up to a consideration of the special Matthean material it will help to note a few passages where Matthew has made significant additions to Mark's text.

Mt 26:42. Matthew has expanded Mk 14:39 into a second prayer of Jesus: 'My Father, if this cannot pass unless I drink it, your will be done.'

26:48b. 'Greetings, Rabbi!' Jesus does not approve of the use of 'rabbi' as a salutation (much less as a title). Judas' use of the term (vv 22, 25) marks him as one already outside the company of Jesus' disciples.

26:51-54. Matthew specifies that he who cut off the ear of the high priest's slave was 'one of those with Jesus.' See Mk 14:47 'one of those who stood near.' Matthew, unlike Mark, records Jesus'

response to the sword-wielder (vv 52-54). The command to put up
the sword is bolstered by a warning. Besides, Jesus does not need
such paltry help: his Father could readily supply 'more than twelve
legions of angels.' See Dan 12:1; 2 Macc 5:2-3; 10:29-30. The scriptures must be fulfilled (vv 54, 56) – see 26:31 (Zech 13:7); 27:46 (Ps
22:2). In Matthew's view God has written from beginning to end
what must be.

26:59. All the gospels agree that the Sanhedrin authorities were
instrumental in having Jesus arrested and in handing him over to
the Romans for sentence of death. Matthew has emphasised the
malevolence of Jewish involvement. In 26:69 the 'chief priests and
the whole council' seek *false* testimony against Jesus (compare Mk
14:55). It is probable that something said or done by Jesus had been
interpreted as a threat to destroy the Temple and would have been
a partial cause of the Sanhedrin's action against Jesus. But Matthew
is proposing conscious vindictiveness.

The Price of Innocent Blood 27:3-10

In 27 1-2 Matthew tells of Jesus being led to Pilate. Then follows the
first of the passages peculiarly his own: Judas and the price of innocent blood (27:3-10). When Judas had agreed to betray Jesus he had
received in payment thirty pieces of silver (26:14-15). Now, full of
remorse, he comes back with the money: 'I have sinned by betray-
ing innocent blood' (27:3-4). He is conscious of a heinous crime (see
Jer 26:15; 2 Kg 24:4). The priests respond callously, 'What is that to
us?' A despairing Judas threw the money into the Temple sanctu-
ary and went and hanged himself – an action reminiscent of
Ahitophel (2 Sam 17:23). The high priests are, willy nilly, contami-
nated by the blood money. Their decision to be rid of it is indirect
acknowledgment of Jesus' innocence: 'It is not lawful to put them in
the treasury, since they are blood money' (v 6) – 'blood money'
being the price of *innocent* blood. The passage ends with the pur-
chase of the Field of Blood (vv 7-8) and a typical Matthean fulfilment citation – this one rather obscure (vv 9-10). Another, notably
different, version of the fate of Judas is found in Acts 1:16-20.
Evidently, there was an early Christian tradition about a sudden
death of Judas. Or, perhaps, a conviction that he must have come to
a sticky end.

The Roman Trial 27:1-26

Matthew's Roman trial is twice as long as the Marcan account. Matthew followed Mark but supplemented the material with further dramatic incidents that enliven the account and heighten the theological import. In the Barabbas incident (27:15-26) some manuscripts have an intriguing reading: 'At that time they had a notorious prisoner, called *Jesus* Barabbas. So after they had gathered, Pilate said to them. "Whom do you want me to release for you, *Jesus* Barabbas or Jesus who is called the Messiah?"' The reading Jesus Barabbas is now widely regarded as authentic – as in the *New Revised Standard Version*. A weighty argument is that, while it is easy to imagine Christian scribes wanting to omit that embarrassing 'Jesus', it is incomprehensible that they should have added it. The Matthean contrast, then, is highly dramatic.

The message of Pilate's wife (27:19) is proper to Matthew. 'While he was sitting on the judgment seat, his wife sent word to him, "Have nothing to do with that innocent man, for today I have suffered a great deal because of a dream about him."' This links up with the Judas story and leads to the episode of Pilate's hand-washing. Indeed, it was his wife's testimony that led Pilate to strive to rid himself of the taint of innocent blood. The dream motif recalls the dreams of Joseph (1:20; 2:13, 19) and of the Magi (2:12) in the infancy narrative.

In 27:23 Pilate declares the innocence of Jesus – as he does three times in Luke and John. This leads to another episode proper to Matthew: Pilate washes his hands (27:24-25). 'He took some water and washed his hands before the crowd saying, "I am innocent of this man's blood; see to it yourselves".' The background is Deuteronomy 21:1-9 – hardly a passage that Pilate would have known! There have been, then, three attempts to evade responsibility for the innocent blood of Jesus. (What is in question is responsibility implied in the story-line, not the actual guilt of those involved).

Despite his gesture with the money Judas could not escape guilt for having set in motion a destructive process that could not be reversed. God's punishment for that guilt was evidenced in Judas' suicide. (This again is the popular estimation). Although the chief priests by rejecting the money tried to escape Judas' transfer of responsibility to them, they were in fact the most responsible for innocent blood because of the death sentence they had just passed on Jesus, after having sought false testimony against him (26:59, 66). Jesus had warned that divine judgment would come upon them (26:64). As for Pilate's attempt to avoid responsibility while passing a sentence on an innocent man, the washing ritual of Deuteronomy 21 is efficacious only if the elders who performed it had no share in the murder either by doing it themselves or knowing who did. Pilate may not have borne the principal responsibility, but he cannot wash himself clean any more than Lady Macbeth can wash out the 'damned spot'.[22]

His Blood Be Upon Us! 27:25

Matthew adds a response to that gesture of Pilate: 'Then the people as a whole answered. "His blood be on us and on our children!"' (27:25). With a well-known biblical formula (see Lev 20:9-16; Josh 2:19-20; 23 Sam 1:16; 14:9; Jer 51:35) Israel accepts responsibility for Jesus' death. Pilate has (to his satisfaction) waived responsibility. He challenged the crowd: 'See to it yourselves,' that is, You shoulder the blame. They, convinced that a Jesus condemned by the Sanhedrin was a blasphemer, do accept responsibility. They act on their discernment of the situation. The phrase, 'and our children', in context, means one generation, that involved in the destruction of Jerusalem and the Temple (see Mt 24:15-21). Historically, this text has had dire consequences for Jews. The comment of Daniel Harrington is apposite:

> Matthew 27:11-26 (and especially 27:25) is a major text in the history and present reality of Christian-Jewish relations. Teachers and preachers have a serious obligation to work through this text with care and objectivity. They must give attention to the conflicting portraits of Pilate in the Gospels and other Jewish sources. They must help others to see Matthew's special interest in the Jewish leaders and crowds and his comparative lack of interest in Pilate. Above all it is necessary to read Mt 27:25 ('His blood be upon us and upon our children') in its Matthean setting, not as applying to all Jews at all times or

just the small percentage of Jews in Jerusalem who involved themselves in Jesus' trial before Pilate. The Matthean setting involves both the time of Jesus and the time after 70 AD, and is rooted in an inner-Jewish quarrel.[23]

Apocalyptic Signs 27:51b-53

The death of Jesus was followed by the rending of the curtain of the Temple – signalling the end of the Temple, or even of the Old Covenant (27:51a). Here Matthew adds four other apocalyptic signs: 'The earth shook and the rocks were split. The tombs also were opened, and many bodies of the saints who had fallen asleep were raised. After his resurrection they came out of the tombs and entered the holy city and appeared to many' (27:51b-53). The whole passage is symbolic and couched in popular poetic terms. The earthquake marks the death of Jesus as an epoch-making event and serves as a prelude to the resurrection of the dead. The rising of 'many bodies' is not the general resurrection. It is a symbol of the inbreaking of God's power signalling the beginning of the last era, and it characterises the death of Jesus as an event that makes possible the resurrection of others. 'After his resurrection' is awkward in its setting. Its purpose is theological: to link the resurrection of the 'saints' with the resurrection of Jesus (and not only with his death). One asks of the passage: What does it mean? – not, Did all this happen?

RESURRECTION 28:1-15

When in 1 Corinthians 15 Paul energetically defends the reality of resurrection from the dead, he starts by appealing to the resurrection of Jesus (15:3-8). It is clear, from the New Testament as a whole, that Christians were, from the first, convinced that the crucified Christ was not held by death. In Jewish faith and prayer, God is he who 'makes the dead live.' Jewish faith and hope looked to a resurrection of the righteous at the end of time. What the first Christians asserted was that, in the person of Jesus of Nazareth, this divine act had taken place. Jewish expectation was eschatological: resurrection was an event of the end-time. Christians had asserted that an eschatological event had taken place in time. If one can put it so, the resurrection of Jesus is an event at once eschatological and historical. In essence it is a spiritual event, beyond our world of time, and yet it has impinged on our world of time. Paul uses the word *óphthé* to state that Christ appeared to Cephas, to the other witnesses listed, and to Paul himself. The word can be rendered 'he showed himself'. It means that the risen Jesus manifested himself as present in some fashion so that Paul, and the others, can say, 'I have seen the Lord.' What is involved is a divine initiative leading to real experience of the presence of the Lord and a firm conviction of the reality of this presence. Something had happened to these men and women which they could only describe by saying that they had 'seen the Lord,' that the Lord had 'shown himself' to them. The phrase did not refer to some general Christian experience but rather to a particular series of occurrences confined to a limited period. Such occurrences, on the threshold of ordinary human experience, just would not submit to precision of detail. Only symbol and imagery, not literal prose, could tell *this* story.

The Narratives

Six gospel passages serve as sources for our knowledge of the resurrection: Mk 16:1-8; Mt 28; Lk 24:13-49; Jn 20; Jn 21; Mk 16:9-20 (and to these should be added Paul's text in 1 Cor 15:5-8). In this group we may distinguish two types of narrative: those of the post-resurrection appearances and those of the finding of the empty tomb. The narratives of the post-resurrection appearances were composed to ground Christian faith in the risen Jesus and to justify apostolic preaching. The nature of such appearances makes it obvious enough that the gospels cannot agree where and to whom Jesus appeared. This diversity does not seriously affect the historicity of the occurrences; it is a product of the manner in which the stories were told and preserved. A constant feature of the resurrection narratives, with the exception of Mt 28 (but note 28:17) is that the Lord is not at once recognised (Lk 24:16, 37; Jn 20:14-15; 21:4). It required some word or some familiar gesture of his to make him known. This is an effective way of making the point that Jesus had not returned to life as before but had passed beyond death to *new* life with God. He is Jesus – and yet he is different. The appearance stories are heavily laden with theological and apologetic motifs.

The Empty Tomb 28:1-15

The women (Mt 28:1) came to 'see' the tomb (and not to anoint the body of Jesus as in Mk 16:1). Here that office is ruled out because of the guard at the tomb. The apocalyptic 'earthquake' (v 2) links the resurrection with the death (27:51-54) as the great eschatological event which ushers in the new age. The 'guards' (v 4) are those of 27:62-66, a passage that is a product of Christian apologetic concern. The interpreting angel addressed his glad tidings to the women: they must not fear but should rejoice because the crucified Jesus they sought is now the Risen One. With joy, they ran to tell the disciples (effectively, the Twelve). Suddenly, Jesus met them. Here, uniquely in stories of encounter with the risen Jesus, he is recognised at once. Fittingly, the women worship this Lord. His message was that they must hasten to announce the good news to the disciples: they will meet Jesus again in Galilee. Go and tell 'my *brothers*', those who had failed him so miserably. It is the graciousness of total forgiveness. The word of God is for all ages; there is surely a message for our day in this passage. *Women* were the first to hear the good news of the resurrection; *women* were the first heralds of the resurrection (vv 7, 10). *Women* were the first to meet the risen Lord – rather, to be met by him! When will the church hearken to this word?

The final special Matthean material is that which specifies guards at the tomb (27:62-66). Matthew's purpose is polemical: to refute a current story that Jesus' disciples had stolen the body and on that basis had proclaimed the resurrection. While it continues into the empty tomb narrative (28:2-4, 11-15), comparison with the other gospels makes clear that the guard story is not historical. After recounting that the guards had been bribed to spread the story that the disciples had stolen the body of Jesus, Matthew observes: 'This story is still told among the Jews to this day' (28:15). The episode has been built into the burial and empty tomb stories as a way of anticipating an objection that is sure to be raised. The tomb was found empty, not because the body had been stolen, but because Jesus had been raised from the dead. But the objection had to be met and a lie nailed.

The Lord of Life

It is evident from our gospels that the resurrection of Jesus is not at all the resuscitation of a corpse in the sense of a return to earthly life. The resurrection of Jesus means his rising to life beyond death. The risen Jesus lives a life that transcends earthly life; he has broken out of the confines of time and place. The risen Jesus was present to his disciples in a new and unfettered manner. And not only to his original disciples; he is present, potentially, to all men and women through time and history. This abiding presence is implied in Mt 28:20: 'I am with you always, to the end of the age.' He is the same Jesus of his earthly life, but now transformed. Paul can declare: 'The last Adam [Christ] became a life-giving Spirit' (1 Cor 15:45), living a Spirit-life now and no longer a life of flesh. Christians came to understand that 'eternal life' is life with God and with the risen Jesus. That conviction is enshrined in the promise to the 'good thief': 'Truly I tell you, today you will be with me in Paradise' (Lk 23:43). Instead of trying to situate or describe 'paradise' it is more profitable to recall the comment of Ambrose: *Vita est enim esse cum Christo: ideo ubi Christus, ibi vita, ibi regnum.* Life means living with Christ. Where Christ is, there too is life and there is the kingdom.

The Great Commission 28:16-20

The disciples went to Galilee as they had been bidden (28:10). There the risen Jesus appeared to them. A 'mountain' is a place of revelation – an apt setting. The 'eleven' adored their Lord – yet some 'doubted': Matthew is drawing for his community a picture of the Christian community: believers caught between adoration and doubt. Jesus solemnly proclaimed that by his death-resurrection he had been granted what had been declared of the Son of Man in Daniel 7:14 – 'To him was given dominion and glory and kingship, that all peoples, nations and languages should serve him.' He was therefore in a position to launch a universal mission. He duly commissioned his representatives who were to achieve his task. Consequently, he sends them into the world to make disciples of 'all nations.' During his ministry Jesus limited his concern to Israel; in this new era the good news is for *all*.

One becomes a *disciple* through baptism in the name of the Father,

Son and Holy Spirit – a triadic formula which doubtless reflects the baptismal liturgy of Matthew's community. The disciples are to teach: to carry on what was a major task of the earthly Jesus in the gospel. Disciples must be taught *Jesus'* commands. Christians do not live by the ten commandments – even though, of course, Jesus' teaching includes much of what was in the Torah. For the Christian, Jesus' word is the ultimate norm of morality. In that word will one discern the will of God.

Finally, we have Jesus' great promise of v 20b: 'And remember, I am with you always, to the end of the age.' Matthew skillfully rounds off his gospel by catching up the Emmanuel (God-with-us) of his prologue (1:23). Matthew does not speak of a 'departure' or of a 'farewell' of Jesus. Rather, he places the community at the heart of the universal power of the resurrection. The 'end of the age' which he has in mind designates the time of the church (see 13:39-40; 24:3). It corresponds to the 'from now on' of 26:64 where Jesus tells Caiaphas: 'From now on you will see the Son of Man seated at the right hand of Power...' Jesus is promising his steadfast help, echoing all his assurances throughout the gospel: Fear not!; I am with you!; It is I! Whereas Luke closes with a farewell blessing and ascension (Lk 24:51) here in Matthew Jesus assures us that he will be abidingly present in the community. Moreover, what is present is not his static presence in one chosen group, but his dynamic and helping presence for a worldwide mission. This promise to be with us always is an encouraging word to the church of our day – a church seemingly lost in a mass of humanity.

> The story concludes on a mountain in Galilee with the gospel turning its face to the future and to the nations. But in a very real sense, it does not conclude at all. Through the final words of Jesus to his disciples, Matthew projects the gospel story out into the time and space of the reader's world, and even farther, to those who would accept the message of Jesus' missionaries, be baptised by them, and through them be schooled in the way of Jesus. Jesus' message to the disciples is now clearly a message directed to the church.[24]

Conclusion

Jesus of Nazareth is one. Christian perception of him varies. The variation is manifest in our gospels. While the works of Mark, Luke and Matthew are closely related, the differences are manifest. These are, in large measure, occasioned by the community situation of each evangelist and by the concerns and needs of that situation. The temperament of each is surely also a factor. Matthew's community was Jewish-Christian. In the stressful days after the traumatic disaster of 70 AD it found itself in a state of cold-war with official Judaism. Its stance was that Jesus is the Teacher who speaks more authoritatively than Moses. This is stressed by Matthew. Arguably, the statement, 'Every scribe who has been trained for the kingdom of heaven is like the master of a household who brings out of his treasures what is new and what is old' (13:52) reflects Matthew's view of himself as something of a Christian sage. At any rate, in his Sermons, he has cast Jesus as the Sage.

Beforehand, in his infancy Narrative, he firmly asserted that Jesus is son of David and son of Abraham: Saviour of Jew and Gentile. At the same time, his ancestry shows him to be wholly one of us, 'like his brothers and sisters in every respect' (Heb 2:17). Virginally conceived, Jesus is God-with-us. Son of David, he was, appropriately, born in Bethlehem. The Gentile Magi acknowledged the king of the Jews. He re-enacted the Exodus of his people and, figurately, suffered their Exile. As 'the Nazarene' he embarked on his mission. The Sermons follow the stages of the mission.

In the Sermon on the Mount Jesus addressed his people; the beatitudes are thoroughly Jewish in form and content. he assured his people that he had not come to abolish Torah and Prophets; he was their prophetic fulfilment. His challenge broadened and deepened the meaning of the term 'righteousness', the doing of God's will.

For the Christian, the ultimate authority is not the Law of Moses but 'these words of mine.'

Jesus was sent 'only to the lost sheep of the house of Israel'. The initial mission of the Twelve had the same limitation. Matthew's community saw itself as the authentic way of Judaism. Mission brings trial. They must maintain trust in God. They and those who hearkened to them will be recompensed by a generous God. Jesus spoke in parables. His purpose was unequivocal: to challenge and teach. Matthew, in the Sermon in Parables, gives the impression that Jesus was reacting to the rejection of his word; his parables were punishment of unfaith. Again, the evangelist displays his preoccupation: the struggle with contemporary Judaism. Paradoxically, in 13:36-52, Jesus encourages his disciples – in parables.

A Christian community needs structure, but there is inherent danger. This is brought out in the Sermon on the Church (ch 18). It is the special duty of leaders to care for the weak and vulnerable; not, through insensitivity, to make their lot harder. All members of a community should display mutual concern, especially where there is need of correction. Forgiveness – 'seventy times seven' – is the hallmark; they are to mirror the conduct of an infinitely forgiving Abba. As for the exercise of authority, chapter 23 shows, eloquently, how it is *not* to be exercised. Jesus had stood authority on its head: *exousia* (authority) is shown in *diakonia* (service). Already, by Matthew's day, Christian leaders were sporting titles and flexing ecclesiastical muscle.

The Judgment Sermon (chs 24-25) uses the prospect of eschatological trials to exhort Christians to respond to present difficulties. Parables figure prominently. The Ten Maidens inculcates watchfulness. The Talents challenges an image of God as exacting taskmaster: it inhibits. The image of a generous God is liberating; one will dare to take risks. The Last Judgment serves as an imperative call to action in the here and now. Jesus' solidarity with all who suffer copper-fastens his image of the gracious God who has preferential option for the poor.

In his Passion, Jesus, abandoned by his followers, faced his hour of trial alone. In Gethsemane he suffered the pain of unanswered

prayer; on Calvary the anguish of Godforsakenness. All the evangelists stress the innocence of Jesus and have Pilate witness to it.
Matthew underlines the fact by presenting the death of Jesus as the
heinous crime of the shedding of innocent blood. This is acknowledged by Judas and the priests and, dramatically, by Pilate in his
futile washing of hands. The Magi had come to seek 'the king of the
Jews'; Jesus died as King of the Jews. The further significance of his
death was marked, symbolically, by apocalyptic sings. The centurion
and his men confessed, in awe: 'Truly this man was God's Son!'

Death was not the end. The women who had come to mourn a dead
Jesus were met by the risen Lord. He gave them a message for his
'brothers' – their failure forgiven. They will see him in Galilee. And
when they met they received the commission: 'Go therefore and
make disciples of all nations.' And the assurance: 'And remember, I
am with you always, to the end of the age.'

Notes

1. Harrington, Wilfrid J., *Mark: Realistic Theologian: The Jesus of Mark; Luke: Gracious Theologian: The Jesus of Luke*, (Dublin: The Columba Press, 1996, 1997).
2. Harrington, Daniel J., 'Matthew as a Jewish Book', *Priests & People* 7 (1993), 242.
3. Senior, Donald, *The Gospel of Matthew*, (Nashville: Abingdon Press, 1997), 53.
4. See Note 1.
5. *The Epistle of Paul to the Romans*, (London: Collins, 1959), 109f.
6. Schüssler Fiorenza, Elizabeth, *In Memory of Her: A Feminist Theological Reconstruction of Christian Origins*, (New York: Crossroad, 1983), xiii.
7. Harrington, Wilfrid, *The Jesus Story*, (Dublin/Collegeville: The Columba Press/The Liturgical Press, 1991), 49f.
8. Meier, John P., *Matthew*. New Testament Message 3. (Wilmington: Michael Glazier, 1980), 3f.
9. One should note that not until the second century BC was there, in Israel, any real notion of an afterlife. Life ended in the gloom of Sheol – effectively, the grave.
10. I acknowledge my indebtedness to the scholarship of Raymond E. Brown: *The Birth of the Messiah*, New Updated Edition (New York: Doubleday, 1993).
11. Harrington, Daniel J., *The Gospel of Matthew*. Sacra Pagina 1. A Michael Glazier Book. (Collegeville: The Liturgical Press, 1991), 84.
12. *The Revelation of St John the Divine* , (London: A & C Black, 1966), 170.
13. For a brief study of miracles and Jesus as healer and exorcist see W. J. Harrington, *Mark: Realistic Theologian*, 73-95.

14. Harrington, D. J., op. cit., 143f.

15. Meier, J. P., op. cit., 128.

16. Kingsbury, Jack D., *The Parables of Jesus in Matthew 13*, (London: SPCK, 1969).

17. See Harrington, W. J., *Mark: Realistic Theologian*, 32-34.

18. Schillebeeckx, Edward, *God Among Us*, (New York: Crossroad, 1993), 62.

19. Brown, Raymond, E., *The Death of the Messiah*. 2 vols. Anchor Bible Reference Library (New York/London: Doubleday/ Geoffrey Chapman, 1994), 27f.

20. Here I follow the relevant lines of R. E. Brown's investigation in his *The Death of the Messiah*. See W. Harrington, 'The Passion' in *The Gracious Word. Year A*. (Dublin: Dominican Publications, 1995), 69-74.

21. R. E. Brown, op. cit., 63.

22. R. E. Brown, op. cit., 836.

23. op. cit., 393.

24. Senior, Donald, op. cit., 177.

For Reference and Further Study

MATTHEW

F. W. Beare, *The Gospel According to Matthew,* (San Francisco: Harper & Row, 1981).

R. E. Brown, 'The Gospel According to Matthew' in *An Introduction to the New Testament,* (New York: Doubleday, 1997), 171-227.

W. D. Davies and D. C. Allison, *The Gospel According to St Matthew,* ICC, 3 vols. (Edinburgh: T. & T. Clark, 1988).

D. J. Harrington, *The Gospel of Matthew,* Sacra Pagina 1. A Michael Glazier Book. (Collegeville: The Liturgical Press, 1991).

J. D. Kingsbury, *Matthew: Structure, Christology, Kingdom* (Philadelphia: Fortress, 1975).

— *Matthew as Story,* (Philadelphia: Fortress, 1988).

J. P. Meier, *Matthew.* New Testament Message 3 (Wilmington: Michael Glazier, 1980).

D. Senior, *The Gospel of Matthew* , (Nashville: Abingdon Press, 1997).

G. N. Stanton, *A Gospel for a New People. Studies in Matthew,* (Edinburgh: T. & T. Clark, 1992).

A. Stock, *The Method and Message of Matthew,* (Collegeville: The Liturgical Press, 1994).

Interpretation, *The Gospel of Matthew,* XLVI, No. 4, 1992.

GENERAL

R. E. Brown, *The Birth of the Messiah,* Updated Edition (New York: Doubleday, 1993).

— *The Death of the Messiah,* 2 vols. (New York/London: Doubleday/ Chapman, 1994).

J. P. Meier, *A Marginal Jew*, vol. 1. *Rethinking the Historical Jesus*, (New York: Doubleday, 1991).

E. P. Sanders, *Jesus and Judaism*, (London: SCM, 1985).

— *The Historical Figure of Jesus*, (London:Penguin Books, 1995).

Index to Matthean Passages

Mark: Realistic Theologian
The Jesus of Mark
Wilfrid J. Harrington OP

Mark is a brilliant storyteller and a thoughtful theologian, one of whose distinctive traits is his realism. Mark's gospel is a theology of the cross, and before the cross there is nowhere to hide. All human life is there.

This book aims to present the Jesus of Mark's faith. Fr Harrington opens with chapters on Mark and on Jesus and then explores the Jesus of this gospel as prophet, as healer, as exorcist, and as Messiah. Finally, he returns to the cross:

> On the cross, Jesus shows what it is to be human ... He shows us that we are truly human when we accept our humanness, when we face up to the fact that we are not masters of our fate ... On its own, humankind has indeed reason to fear. With God, in total dependence on God, there is no place for fear. The resurrection of Jesus makes that clear.

This clear, simply written book will be invaluable to all who preach, teach or simply want to understand better the gospel of Mark.

ISBN 1 85607 169 3   152 pages   £8.99

Also available from Columba

Luke: Gracious Theologian
The Jesus of Luke
Wilfrid J. Harrington OP

The gospel of Luke is the gospel that portrays Jesus most clearly as Saviour. It is in this gospel that we find a Jesus of sensitivity and compassion. There is great gentleness, but there is nothing soft or easy-going about this Jesus. On the other hand, he does reflect the God who is, disconcertingly, the God of sinners. The Lucan Jesus, who truly knows the Father, is wholly in the business of lifting the burden of sin – not of adding to it.

Luke believes that what Jesus did, said, and suffered had and has a significance for and bearing on human history. Luke does not seek to suppress the tragedy and mystery of the cross nor undervalue its saving role. He does not question the need for the disciple of Jesus to deny the self, to take up the cross, and follow the Master.

Luke has shown what may be made of Jesus' deeds and words in a time after the era of Jesus. For us in the twentieth century, conscious of a gap of two millennia between the first proclamation of the Christian message and our striving to assimilate that message, Luke's preaching of the good news may be more congenial than others.

ISBN 1 85607 206 1   120 pages   £8.99

Also available from Columba

The Jesus Story

Wilfrid J. Harrington OP

Why do we have *four* gospels? After all, Jesus Christ is one person who lived one life. The fact is that none of the evangelists is primarily interested in presenting a biography of Jesus of Nazareth. Each is, in the first place, addressing a Christian community, with the concerns and the needs of that community in mind. His readers knew the basic Jesus story as well as the evangelist. He makes his point by telling the story in *his* way.

This book hits on the novel expedient of having Jesus, the dominant character in each gospel, tell his story in his own words – a story which sounds different in each gospel. The introductory chapter makes clear that the approach, while not aimed at scholars, follows the line of modern scholarly understanding of the gospels.

ISBN 0 948183 93 4   166 pages   £8.99